Links to Literature

Links to Literature:

Teaching Tools to Enhance Literacy, Character and Social Skills

Rosemary Lonberger

Jane Harrison

esr

EDUCATORS FOR SOCIAL RESPONSIBILITY

Links to Literature: Teaching Tools to Enhance Literacy, Character and Social Skills

By Rosemary Lonberger and Jane Harrison
© 2008 Educators for Social Responsibility

esr

EDUCATORS FOR SOCIAL RESPONSIBILITY
Educators for Social Responsibility, Inc.
23 Garden St.
Cambridge, MA 02138
www.esrnational.org

Cover design by John Barnett / 4 Eyes Design
Book design by Erin Dawson

10 9 8 7 6 5 4 3 2 1
Printed in the United States of America

ISBN 13: 978-0-942349-24-5

ACKNOWLEDGEMENTS:

From Rosemary: The publication of this book would not have happened if it wasn't for key individuals and organizations. I was surrounded by people who provided love and assistance all of whom I hold in high regard. First, I would like to thank Larry Dieringer who was patient with me and didn't lose faith in my potential. I also thank Jeff Perkins who was the first person to say, "This looks like a book", and Rachel Poliner who introduced me to the Stories Program at ESR. My dear friend Sharon kept me organized throughout the writing of the text, and Marion Barnett watched over me spiritually. Buffalo State College and the Office of Organized Research granted me the sabbatical I needed to do most of the work on the manuscript. Thanks to all of the reading researchers whose shoulders on which I stand. Finally and most importantly, I would like to thank my dad, who always believes I can succeed at anything I try.

From Jane: Many thanks to Audra Longert for shepherding the project so successfully, and Sam Diener who moved the project along during his time at ESR. To my dear friend and colleague Ken Breeding for consistently being supportive, helpful, and full of wonderful insights; and to Denise Wolk who brought her vision and new thinking to ESR. Thanks also to Carol Spiegel for her many contributions of books in the Links to Literature in each chapter. As always, my work is dedicated to my family who support me every day with love and encouragement.

ESR wishes to express deep gratitude to William (Bill) Kreidler and Rachel Poliner for their pioneering work teaching conflict resolution and social and emotional competencies through literature and language arts. One of the early leaders in the field of conflict resolution education, Bill first showed teachers how to bring his practical and creative approach to the world of literature in *Teaching Conflict Resolution Through Children's Literature* (1994). Bill took great joy in reading books aloud to adults and children, and playfully but clearly drew out the conflict resolution lesson. Rachel extended this work by creating a large collection of tools for helping children develop social and emotional skills. She worked extensively with schools to integrate the tools into their existing literature and language arts programs. Rachel also founded and managed an ESR program that gave an annual award to a children's book author whose work exemplifies the integration of social themes and social responsibility into literature.

· · · · · · · · · · · · · ·

ESR is deeply grateful to the following foundations for their support of the development and production of this guide: The Susan A. and Donald P. Babson Charitable Foundation, Compton Foundation, Inc., The William and Flora Hewlett Foundation, and the Lippincott Foundation of the Peace Development Fund.

Contents

Introduction

Social and emotional learning is not a new concept. Many teachers have instinctively realized the importance of providing a respectful, caring classroom environment where students learn to work well with each other, manage their emotions, and learn about the larger world and their connection to it. Daniel Goleman's 1995 book, *Emotional Intelligence*, brought social and emotional issues to the forefront of educational discourse and proposed that social and emotional competencies contribute more to success than what has traditionally been called "intelligence." Goleman and other researchers in this field confirmed what teachers knew all along: effective students need to be emotionally and socially "literate."

What are these social and emotional skills? Communicating effectively, working cooperatively with others, managing emotions appropriately, perspective-taking, showing empathy, and resolving conflict creatively and nonviolently. When academic and social and emotional learning both become a part of school, students are more likely to remember and use what they are taught. They also incorporate into their education a sense of responsibility, caring, and concern for the well-being of others, as well as themselves.

CASEL, the Collaborative for Academic, Social and Emotional Learning, reminds us that a growing body of research corroborates the connection between social and emotional learning and academic success. Social and emotional learning has been found to improve academic attitudes (motivation and commitment), behaviors (attendance, study habits, cooperative learning) and performance (grades, test scores, and subject mastery) (Zins et al., 2004). Based on evidence from 61 educational researchers, 91 meta-analyses, and 179 handbook chapters, Wang, Haertel, and Wallberg (1997) found that social and emotional factors were among the most influential factors on student learning.

Integrating social and emotional learning with academic instruction is a particularly effective way of promoting both social-emotional and academic competence. For instance, when students are asked to use SEL skills such as perspective-taking and problem solving to understand and analyze historical events or stories in a language arts class, learning in these content areas improves (Elias, 2004). Another program exposes students to a high-quality reading and language arts curriculum drawn from diverse cultures. This intervention encourages students to explore the values and behaviors of characters in a wide variety of fictional situations, and teaches them to consider the needs and perspectives of others (Schaps, Battistich, & Solomon, 2004). Findings from a program evaluation in 24 school districts revealed that the intervention positively impacted students' attitudes, motives, and ethical values. Most remarkable among the findings was that students in schools where the intervention was well implemented outperformed comparison students on district achievement tests and achieved higher grade point averages in a four-year follow-up study. Preliminary findings from another recently released program from these same program developers that incorporates cooperative learning techniques into the reading curriculum indicated that students' reading comprehension scores were significantly improved after the first year. (SEL & Academics, 2007)

The difficult question that arises for all of us who work with students is how to find the time to provide this skill building for our students. It's not that we haven't recognized the need to do so; most teachers are well aware that their students seem to actually be *less* socially skilled than previous generations and research cited in *Emotional Intelligence* bears this out. We can attribute this to many possible theories: busier lives with less parental contact, children's preoccupation with media that require no personal interaction, less time spent with others in play. Theories, though, can't help us change the fact that our students are coming to school less socially skilled, and less connected with other students and to the school environment.

So what is there to do — especially in a climate of high-stakes testing — to provide experiences that build more emotional and social skills and create a classroom where everyone feels a connection to each other and to school? We hope that this book might provide an answer to this dilemma. In it, you'll find numerous ways to link literature and literacy standards with social and emotional learning. Children's literature is a powerful medium for teaching these skills. Engaging in literature is an emotional experience that can hold students' interest while widening their perspective and allowing them to explore feelings, of both the self and others. Think for a moment about the books you have read, and how they have broadened your horizons and expanded your world. Maybe they changed the way you see yourself, or your culture, or the culture of others. Our students are hungry to explore their world and figure out where they fit. Literature can provide a wonderful opportunity to do this.

Each chapter in this book provides specific tools that address social and emotional skills along with ways to introduce them in the classroom. Examples of how to use each tool with specific pieces of literature follow. Other books may certainly be used; those cited here are used for examples and have been chosen because they are well loved by students and provide a wide range of experiences for students to explore. At the conclusion of each chapter, further titles are listed for additional practice with the tools

One thing to consider as you begin to use these tools: Even if a book is identified as an early elementary book, don't dismiss the possibility of its being very effective with older students. Upper-elementary students can be very responsive to picture books. These books provide a connection to an earlier, and generally happier time for students. They have strong themes, and are easily used to explore issues that are important to the lives of all students.

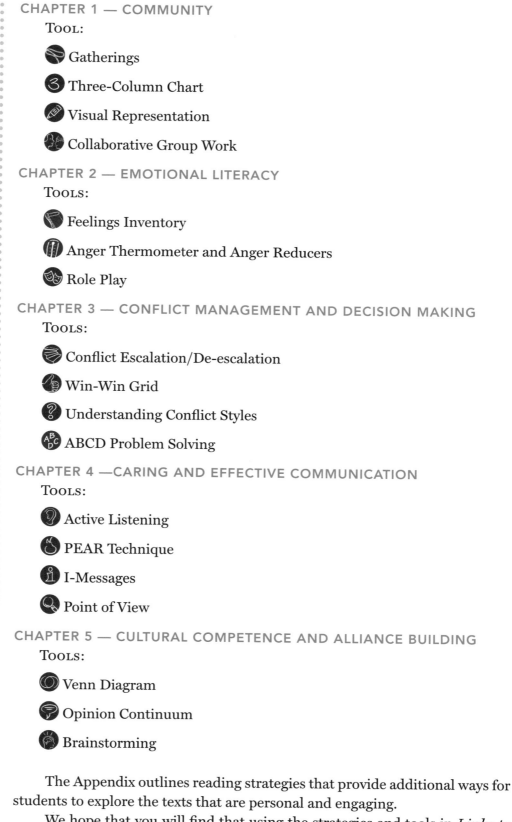
The Appendix outlines reading strategies that provide additional ways for students to explore the texts that are personal and engaging.

We hope that you will find that using the strategies and tools in *Links to Literature* useful in creating a rich and productive community in your classroom.

Chapter 1

Building Community

The experience of participating as a contributing member of a community is an important element in students' learning. Many students grow up with little sense of neighborhood community; increasingly, they spend many hours watching television and using the computer. Some students may not be allowed to play outdoors, and can feel isolated even when they live in urban areas surrounded by people. Without as many face-to-face social interactions, many students have limited opportunities to learn to work cooperatively and to problem solve with others. Creating a successful classroom community will enable teachers to address these crucial aspects of students' social, emotional, and cognitive development.

A successful classroom community is formed by bringing together individuals with unique lives and experiences, different interests, and varying levels of abilities, and creating a unified group whose common goals include relating positively to others, as well as becoming successful learners. Abraham Maslow's hierarchy of needs, outlined in his *Theory of Human Motivation, (1943)* stresses that having one's basic emotional needs met creates the foundation for building higher levels of knowledge and understanding. A classroom community in which students relate well to each other and become successful learners, is also meeting the basic emotional needs of safety and belonging.

These goals require the students, as well as the teacher, to turn their classroom into an efficient, caring community where students feel safe and connected to each other, and academic success can develop and thrive. In such a community, students can increase their emotional and social competencies and take ownership of creating a respectful learning environment. Students, as human beings, wish to be part of a welcoming, supportive community regardless of grade level or whether they live in an urban or rural setting. They want to find friends and make connections with the people around them. As Thomas Lickona reminds us in *Educating for Character,*

> *[Children] need to be in a community – to interact, form relationships, work out problems, grow as a group, and learn directly, from their first hand experience, lessons about fair play, cooperation, forgiveness, and respect for the worth and dignity of every individual (Lickona, 1992, 90).*

The tools introduced in this chapter that will aid in building a connected, high-functioning community include:

- Gathering
- Three-Column Chart
- Visual Representation
- Collaborative Group Work

Tool: Gathering

Gatherings are five- to ten-minute activities that encourage positive community building by allowing students to share their experiences with one another in a safe and fun way. They begin with a question or a prompt, to which students then respond. Gatherings can help children affirm their positive qualities, appreciate individual differences, and share emotions. If the activity involves sharing emotions or personal experiences, it is important to give students the opportunity to pass. Gathering formats can include:

- Go-Rounds — each student responds, in turn, to a starting prompt such as: *Name a favorite pet.*

- Popcorn Sharing — volunteers respond to the prompt in random order.

At the beginning of the year, or during the first few times the class is together, keep prompts and questions fairly impersonal. Students will be more forthcoming when they know there is little risk of negative comments by their peers. When beginning a Gathering, remind students to be respectful of everyone's comments and to listen carefully to each other.

How to Use the Gathering Tool

- Ask students to share the title of a book they read and why they liked it.

- When beginning a discussion about literature, ask students to share their opinions about a topic the book addresses. For example, *"Have you ever saved up your money to buy something? If so, what?"*

- Ask students to choose a character from a book the class is reading and identify a quality they share with him or her.

- Ask students to respond to prompts that require them to draw inferences from the reading. For example, *"Share an idea about how you think the main character is feeling about his situation."* Follow up with a personal connection, perhaps on the following day: *"How would you feel if this situation happened to you? Have you ever experienced anything like this?"*

Tool: Three-Column Chart

The Three-Column Chart is used to help students describe specific behaviors related to a concept and to draw inferences about the feelings these behaviors evoke. This is a particularly useful tool to use to begin a discussion with students about how to create a caring community.

Place this chart on the board or on chart paper:

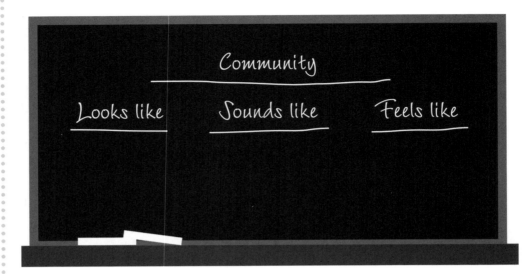

As a way to introduce the three-column chart, provide different definitions of *community* from social studies or science textbooks, or the dictionary. Cite examples of class projects that students have completed and ask why and how each one showed community. Choose a book that illustrates the traits of a caring community. (Suggested titles are cited at the end of this chapter.) Before reading it, ask students to listen for behaviors that illustrate what *community* looks like and sounds like in the story. Elicit answers and fill in the chart. For example, under the *Looks like* column, ask them to describe behavior from the text and pictures that illustrate how community looks in this particular story, such as neighbors helping each other. Elicit quotes directly from the story to complete the *Sounds like* column.

The *Feels like* column of the chart gives students the opportunity to draw inferences about how the specific behaviors identified might make them feel. For example, students might notice that the main character feels happy when others in the community are kind to her. Students may need to examine pictures from the text and have portions of the text reread to them in order to complete the three-column chart.

In the primary grades, the teacher can record students' responses. In later grades, students can record their responses in groups and then groups can share responses during a class discussion. After completing the three-column chart, ask students what behaviors from the story could help their classroom become a caring community. Add responses to the chart and post it in the classroom.

How to Use the Three-Column Chart Tool

- Explore character traits with a three-column chart. Label the chart with the trait (such as *loyalty*), read a selection, and then elicit what loyalty looked like and sounded like in that selection and how this trait would make the other characters feel.

- To personalize a reading, direct students to ask themselves how they might feel in a character's position, and to complete a three-column chart. For example, if a character is the victim of an oppressive act, students can reflect on what the situation would look like, sound like, and feel like.

- When issues arise that are difficult for students to deal with, ask them to picture their classroom as more caring and happy. Complete a three-column chart describing this imaginary community. This process can remind students of the behaviors that contribute to a happy environment without eliciting blaming and defensiveness.

Tool: Visual Representation

Creating a visual end product is a helpful way for many students to see and understand things more deeply. Including a visual learning modality when you are exploring literature enables visual learners to focus on meaning, recognize and group similar ideas easily, and make better use of their visual memory.

A visual way for students to see themselves as contributing members of a community is to create a Class Puzzle. Create one puzzle piece for each student and ask them to write their name and list a positive attribute that they bring to the class. Post the puzzle pieces so they interlock to form a whole image. The final product is a visual reminder that all students are valued individual members of the classroom community.

How to Use the Visual Representation Tool

- Other class projects can include a class quilt and a class apple tree. For the quilt, have each student create his own square of the quilt out of paper or fabric. Combine all the squares to create a quilt. For the apple tree, have each student list an interesting fact about himself on a paper cutout of an apple. Create the tree trunk and branches on a bulletin board. Hang the apples from the tree.

- Students can create a visual representation of the characters in a story that reflects the ways the characters support each other through words or actions. For example, if two characters show kindness to a third, the two would be visually represented as supports to the third.

- Ask students to imagine the setting of the story and draw what it looks like, using information from the text.

- Use this tool to create *before* and *after* visuals for selections that students are reading. This will help students read texts more closely, and encourage them to look for details. For example, before and after the climax of a story – how have characters changed?

Tool: Collaborative Group Work

Allowing students to work in groups provides an opportunity for everyone to feel valued. There are a number of excellent resources that provide structures for facilitating cooperative learning groups, such as *Cooperation in the Classroom* (VI ed.), by Johnson, Johnson, and Holubec (1993), and *Cooperative Learning Structures for Classbuilding*, by Kagan, Robertson, and Kagan (1995). Well-facilitated groups allow for:

- **Positive interdependence**
  Students need each other to complete the assigned task. Teachers can structure interdependence by establishing mutual group goals, offering joint rewards, and providing opportunities to share resources and assigned roles.

- **Individual accountability**
  Each student's performance is frequently assessed, and the results are shared with the group and the individual. This can be achieved through individual assessments or by randomly assigning one member of the group to provide a group answer.

- **Face-to-face interactions**
  Students help each other learn by sharing and encouraging efforts to learn. Students explain, discuss, and teach what they know to classmates. Teachers structure assignments that encourage students to collaborate, including structuring the physical environment to allow students to converse with one another easily.

- **Interpersonal skills**
  The group learns and practices social skills. These skills must be taught as purposefully and precisely as academic skills. Collaborative skills include leadership, decision making, trust building, communication, and conflict management.

- **Reflection /Assessment**
  Groups need time to reflect on how well they are achieving their goals and maintaining effective working relationships among members. Teachers structure group processing skills by assigning group roles, monitoring groups, providing feedback on how well groups are working together, and most importantly, encouraging group reflection. Group performance is evaluated through suggested assessment questions.

How to Use the Collaborative Group Work Tool

Instead of assigning individual projects, choose a project that students can work on in a collaborative group. Divide students into groups in which there are varying levels of ability. The size of each group will depend on the task and the developmental level of the students. It can be helpful to start students in pairs and gradually increase group size.

Take a few minutes to brainstorm with the class and post a list of guidelines to follow while working together. Assign a role to each group member. Although roles may seem contrived at first, they provide a basis for future successful social interactions. Assigned roles will eventually become obsolete because all group members will have assimilated and practiced the elements of each role in their group interactions. Both academic and social roles can be assigned for the same cooperative learning experience. Roles do not have to remain the same each time; they can be varied as needed.

SAMPLE ROLES for **YOUNGER STUDENTS**

Social Roles

TELLER: Tells people when it is their turn and makes sure that everyone has a turn.

CHECKER: Checks each person by asking, "Do you understand the answer?" or "Do you agree with that answer?"

HAPPY TALKER: Encourages and praises people, "That's good," "Thanks, that helps," "We're a great group," etc.

Academic Roles

READER: Reads the task to the group.

WRITER: Records group responses.

REPORTER: Shares the group's answer with the whole class and answers questions.

Examples of additional academic roles might be illustrator, graph-maker, etc.

SAMPLE ROLES for **OLDER STUDENTS**

Social Roles

ENCOURAGER: Encourages all members of the group to share ideas and to work hard. Keeps the group moving through difficult times.

CHECKER: Makes sure that all members agree with the answer and understand the work. Checks feelings.

OBSERVER: Records interactions on an observation sheet. Does not get involved in the task; focuses on group's processing skills.

PRAISER: Praises the group for hard work or for finishing a question. Praises individuals for sharing, helping, listening, and checking.

Academic Roles

DISCUSSION LEADER: Begins conversation by restating task and keeps the discussion focused.

RECORDER: Records group answers.

ACTIVE LISTENER: Listens to students' ideas and responds to what they say. Paraphrases answers in order to be sure that everyone understands.

Reflection/Assessment

At the conclusion of a collaborative group experience, it is helpful to provide time for students to assess how well the group worked together. Individual group members should evaluate their performance in their role, and also assess the performance of the group.

Assessment for young children can consist of asking questions like:

- Can everyone explain the following?

- Name two ways you worked well together.

- Name two ways you could work better together.

Assessment for older students can be more sophisticated:

- What are some of the ways each person in your group participated or contributed?

- Can each group member explain the group's results?

- What did each group member do to carry out his or her role?

- What made it difficult to work together? What did you do about these challenges?

- How could your group have worked together to be more effective? What skills will you use in the future?

- What will you do to help the group work more effectively next time? What skill would you like to work on? (You may keep this skill to yourself if you wish. Next time you work in a group, you can think about whether or not you have shown improvement.)

LINKS TO LITERATURE

A Chair for My Mother

Vera B. Williams

New York: HarperTrophy, 1984 • Grade Level: K-3

Rosa, her mother, and her grandmother lose all of their belonging when a fire destroys their apartment. The family saves their coins in a big jar to purchase the chair they've always dreamed of. It takes a long time, but as a result of their efforts they can finally afford to buy the chair. The neighborhood community also comes to their aid and donates furnishings to help them begin a new life in a new apartment.

 Gathering Tool: Ask students to share a time when others have helped them with a problem. Or have them respond to the prompt: *How would you feel if you had an experience like Rosa's?*

 Three-Column Chart Tool: Create a three-column chart that asks what community *looks like* and *sounds like* in the story, using specific details. Complete the *feels like* section by asking students how they think Rosa felt as a result of her neighbors' actions.

 Visual Representation Tool: Review the acts of caring that the characters in the book show to Rosa and her family. In groups, ask students to create a picture of the community that reflects the interdependence of its members.

 Collaborative Group Work Tool: Divide students into groups and assign roles. Have groups brainstorm ways they could be helpful community members in their neighborhoods. If appropriate, encourage them to contact community agencies to ascertain what they could do that would be most helpful to the community. Each group can then create a list of possible activities, and then narrow the list to one that they will all commit to. Allow time for students to share their completed projects. Ask students to assess how well the group worked together.

Somebody Loves You, Mr. Hatch

Eileen Spinelli

New York: Aladdin Paperbacks, 1996 • Grade Level: K-4

Mr. Hatch is a lonely man who keeps to himself until he receives a large heart-shaped box of chocolates on Valentine's Day from an anonymous person. The attached note reads, "Somebody Loves You." Mr. Hatch suddenly views the world differently because he feels that someone cares about him. His behavior changes as he wonders who his secret admirer could be. As he becomes more extroverted, he is more aware of the needs of others, and shares his time and talents as an active member of his community. The community responds in kind when Mr. Hatch needs them most.

 Gathering Tool: Ask students to respond to this prompt in a Go-Round: *Share a time when someone was helpful to you and you felt that they cared about you.* Follow up the next day, or week, with: *Share a time when you were helpful to someone else, and you let them know that they were important. It might be something you said, or an act of kindness that you did.*

 Three-Column Chart Tool: Elicit direct quotes that describe what community *sounds like* and *looks like* in the story, and have students infer what community *feels like*. A useful next step is to ask which of these behaviors would be helpful for the students' own classroom community.

Visual Representation Tool: Ask groups of students to create illustrations of how the neighbors affected Mr. Hatch's life. Challenge older students to illustrate the changes in Mr. Hatch's behavior when he found out someone cared about him.

Collaborative Group Work Tool: Form groups of students and assign roles. Ask each group to brainstorm a list of valued members of their school and neighborhood communities. Students can choose which person they will honor with an act of appreciation. Have each group share the person they chose, their ideas for showing appreciation and, when completed, their final act of appreciation. Groups can choose to do acts anonymously, as in the book. Ask students to reflect on how their group worked together.

The Summer My Father was Ten

Pat Brisson

Honesdale, PA: Boyds Mills Press, 1999 • Grade Level: K-4

A father tells his young daughter the story of Mr. Bellavista, an Italian immigrant who lived in the father's neighborhood when he was young. Although Mr. Bellavista kept to himself, the neighborhood boys often taunted him because of his accent. Each year, Mr. Bellavista cleared debris from a vacant lot and planted a garden, spending hours caring for the garden. One day, a group of neighborhood boys vandalized the garden, pulled up the vegetables, and threw them at surrounding buildings. The father admits to his daughter that he was one of the boys who destroyed the garden, and although he was sorry for his actions, he could not bring himself to apologize to Mr. Bellavista. It was not until the following year, when Mr. Bellavista refused to plant his garden, that the father apologized. When he offered to help Mr. Bellavista replant the garden, the two began a friendship that lasted for years.

 Gathering Tool: Ask students to tell about a time when they knew they had made a mistake, but found it hard to apologize.

 Three-Column Chart Tool: Using a three-column chart, ask students what the initial community looked like, sounded like, and felt like, and what made it so unhappy for Mr. Bellavista. Create another chart that reflects the changes that occurred after the apology.

 Visual Representation Tool: Work with students to portray the divisiveness of the characters in the story, and then the positive outcome in a "before" and "after" representation. For example, the "before" representation might portray all of the actions of the characters that led Mr. Bellavista to choose not to replant his garden. The "after" representation could portray the changes that needed to occur to create a sense of community between the characters.

 Collaborative Group Work Tool: Divide students into groups and assign roles. Ask each group to brainstorm their possible responses if they had been the neighbors who witnessed the actions against Mr. Bellavista. Ask groups to predict how the plot might have changed as a result of these responses, and to create a story that reflects the changes to share with the class. Allow time for groups to reflect on how well they worked together.

The Color of My Words

Lynn Joseph

New York: HarperTrophy, 2002 • Grade Level: 3+

Twelve-year-old Ana Rosa is a passionate writer who lives in the Dominican Republic. Undaunted by being labeled different by the villagers, as well as by the dangers of living in a country where words are suppressed, she writes about her experiences, her loving family, and the interconnectedness of a caring community. The culture and spirit of life in the Dominican Republic come alive through Ana Rosa's words.

 Gathering Tool: Ask students to share a time when their family or a friend stood by them when others were unkind. Additional prompts could be: *Share a time when you felt no one listened to your concern,* or *Describe a time when you wished that others had come to your aid.*

 Three-Column Chart Tool: *The Color of My Words* depicts life in an exotic locale that is lush and brightly colored. Ask students to complete a three-column chart of the Dominican Republic that depicts their impressions of this environment.

Visual Representation Tool: Create a visual image of a child isolated from her peers because of her differences, a village at odds with its government, and the caring community of Ana Rosa's family.

 Collaborative Group Work Tool: Divide students into groups and assign roles. Ask each group to determine something in their own lives that means a great deal to them, something similar to how Ana Rosa felt about her family's owning their own land. Have each group speak about their issue in the same poetic form that Ana Rosa used. Allow time for students to assess how well their group worked together.

Hana's Suitcase

Karen Levine

Morton Grove, IL: Albert Whitman & Company, 2003 • Grade Level: 4+

Hana's Suitcase is the true story of the Holocaust as seen through a child's eyes. It is also the story of Fumika Ishioka, curator of the Tokyo Holocaust Center, and a group of children known as "Small Wings." The story begins in the year 2000, when a suitcase arrives at the Tokyo Holocaust Center. The suitcase is empty, but the following words are painted on it in white: *Hana Brady; May 16, 1931*; and *Waisenkind*, the German word for orphan. The author alternates chapters between Ishioka's research to locate Hana, and the biography of Hana's life that was recreated as a result of the research. The story ends when Hana's brother is located and comes to the Holocaust Center to share his family's story.

 Gathering Tool: Ask students to respond to the prompt: *What would be most important for you to take with you if you had to leave home? What would you put in your suitcase?*

 Three-Column Chart Tool: Fumika was curious about the name on Hana's suitcase, and her curiosity led to the research that resulted in telling Hana's story. Ask students to create a three-column chart illustrating Fumika's experience. What did the research look like (what occurred), sound like (what might the questions that she needed to ask sound like), and how do the students think she feels as a result of the book's being published?

 Visual Representation Tool: Ask students to draw an object that depicts something in Hana's life. For example, a picture of her home and village prior to German occupation, a Jewish star, Hana's deportation papers, or her drawings from the concentration camp. Place the drawings in a suitcase, or in a display on the wall of the classroom.

 Collaborative Group Work Tool: Divide students into groups and assign roles. Ask each group to choose an object that is meaningful in the story to share in a presentation to the class or another class if possible. The object can be one that was created in the Visual Representation Tool above, or one that is newly created by the group. Each group will need to rehearse a presentation that tells about the object they have chosen. Allow time for group reflection.

ADDITIONAL BOOKS

Swimmy

Leo Lionni

New York: Dragonfly Books, 1973
Grade Level: K-2

Swimmy is the only fish in his family born black instead of red. When he outswims a big fish that devours the rest of this family, he is left all alone. When he least expects it, Swimmy stumbles across another group of small red fish, and his quick thinking helps them to band together to fight the big fish in the sea.

The Best Kind of Gift

Kathi Appelt

New York: HarperCollins, 2003
Grade Level: K-2

When the congregation has a pounding (each person brings a pound of something) to welcome Brother Harper to the community, Jory Timmons feels bad that he cannot give gifts like those (milk, pie, eggs, etc.) from his family. In the end, Jory gives a gift from his heart — a bag of skipping stones.

How to Lose All Your Friends

Nancy Carlson

New York: Puffin Books, 1997
Grade Level: K-3

By humorously describing obnoxious behaviors not wanted in a friend, the author helps students infer the qualities it takes to be a good friend and member of a caring community.

Ruby the Copycat

Peggy Rathmann

New York: Scholastic Paperbacks, 1993
Grade Level: K-3

Ruby, a new student, thinks she must copy another student to be accepted. When she reveals a unique talent that impresses her classmates, she realizes that her uniqueness makes her a valued member of the community.

Nine Animals and the Well

James Rumford

Boston: Houghton Mifflin, 2003
Grade Level: K-3

This is a cumulative tale in which animals meet as they travel to the birthday party for the raja-king. Each time the group meets up with the next animal, that animal has enough gifts for each of them to take a better gift to the raja-king, and they discard their old gifts. At the end they lose everything and the raja-king assures them he just wants their company.

Morning Glory Monday

Arlene Aldo

Toronto: Tundra Books, 2003
Grade Level: K-3

In an effort to cheer up her depressed mother, a little girl plants a morning glory seed that grows, helps her mother, and changes the whole neighborhood and city.

Nora's Ark

Natalie Kinsey-Warnock

New York: HarperCollins, 2005
Grade Level: K-4

Wren's grandparents, Nora and Horace, have nearly finished building their new house when the 1927 Vermont flood comes. The neighbors and their animals arrive with provisions, and the community waits out the flood in the house, built on high ground.

The Goat Lady

Jane Bregoli

Gardiner ME: Tilbury House, 2005
Grade Level: 2-4

The townspeople are skeptical of Noelie, a mysterious old woman who raises goats and other animals. Then the narrator and her brother meet Noelie and discover her kindness. When their mother features Noelie in an art exhibit and people get to know her, they begin to appreciate and respect her. The story is based on the life of Noelie Lemire Houle, who was born in Quebec in 1899.

Danitra Brown, Class Clown

Nikki Grimes

New York: HarperCollins, 2005
Grade Level: 3-5

Zuri Jackson worries about her classes and her own abilities, but her best friend, Danitra Brown, is always there to encourage and support her.

The Harmonica

Tony Johnston

Watertown, MA: Charlesbridge, 2004
Grade Level: 3-6

The Harmonica is the true story of Henryk Rosmaryn, a Polish Jew, who was sent to a concentration camp. When he was ordered to play Schubert on his harmonica for the commandant, he found his real inspiration from the other prisoners, who listened from a distance.

Chapter 2

Emotional Literacy

Developing empathy with others, being aware of one's own feelings, and developing skills to manage those feelings are all aspects of emotional literacy that are critical to becoming a healthy, productive adult. Because many young people have difficulty identifying and naming the feelings they experience, they may not be able either to express accurately how they feel, or to acknowledge the feelings of others. Learning the skills of emotional literacy enables students to express and respond to feelings in healthy and appropriate ways. These skills are helpful as they learn to participate in the classroom, and are useful as well in their personal lives. They are particularly necessary for resolving conflicts successfully, and for creating a harmonious and productive classroom community.

In Daniel Goleman's *Emotional Intelligence*, Goleman cites a great deal of research that concludes that emotions are a key element in the learning process, and that, in fact, emotions drive learning. The research suggests that people who manage their own feelings well and deal constructively with others are more likely to live contented lives, and are also more apt to retain information than those who do not have the skills to manage their emotions successfully. Students' feelings influence their capacity to pay attention: when they can't pay attention, they can't focus, and without focus, they can't commit information to memory. Educating the "heart" by welcoming feelings and emotional energy into the classroom helps teachers educate the mind.

Howard Gardner, Ron Slaby, Daniel Goleman, and other researchers have generally agreed that emotional intelligence has several important aspects:

- **Emotional Awareness of Self and Others** — Students who are able to name their own feelings and discern the feelings of others usually do better in school and in life.

- **Managing Emotions** — Students need appropriate ways to manage feelings. Feelings are not good or bad; it's how one handles them that makes the difference. When students are aware of the intensity of their feelings, they can respond more effectively.

- **Handling Relationships** — Students need to develop skills of resolving interpersonal conflicts, negotiating relationships, and communicating their feelings and needs.

- **Using Emotions Productively** — Intense emotions can make students hate or love, hurt or heal. When students are hopeful, feel safe, respected, and cared for, they are more likely to transform their struggles and setbacks into positive action.

The following tools, presented in this chapter, will help students develop a feelings vocabulary, identify and describe their own feelings, and recognize and respond to their feelings in a manner that contributes to healthy relationships:

- Feelings Inventory
- Anger Thermometer and Anger Reducers
- Role-Play

Tool: Feelings Inventory

The Feelings Inventory helps students develop a feelings vocabulary, take inventory of their emotions, and describe how they are feeling in specific, rather than general terms. A comprehensive feelings inventory is provided on page 31–32. Use it to help create one appropriate for your classroom.

Some teachers like to create their own list of feelings words or have the students generate a list as a class. *Today I Feel Silly*, by Jamie Lee Curtis, and *How Are You Peeling? Foods with Moods,* by Saxton Freymann and Joost Elffers, can be used to generate a feelings inventory with the class. As you read, ask students to listen for feelings words. Then brainstorm a list of feelings words from the story. If students have difficulty remembering specific words, let them refer to the text. When the list is complete, ask if they know any words that mean the same as the words they have generated. Review the meanings of the words on the list, as there may be students who are unfamiliar with some of the feelings words and their synonyms. Display the completed list in the classroom and/or add them to a word wall. (See page 94 for more on Word Walls.) Younger students may need illustrations to increase their word knowledge, and may use the pictures of characters to generate feelings words.

Encourage students to take responsibility for their feelings and to practice using the words from the Feelings Inventory. Suggest that instead of saying, "Joey made me feel upset," for example, students say, "I feel upset." This change of sentence structure can also be a change in the way the student thinks of his ability to manage and modify how he feels.

How to Use the Feelings Inventory Tool

- As you read new books, create an inventory of feelings words, including feelings that are expressly used in the texts and those inferred from a character's actions and words. Have students research the meanings of any words they don't know. Younger students can draw the feelings.

- Show students illustrations and pictures from various stories that depict different emotions. Ask: *What do you think this person is feeling?* Record the words as students say them. Probe for synonyms when possible. If one student says that the person in the picture looks "happy," ask if anyone knows another word for happy that describes this feeling more precisely.

- Use the worksheet "Finding the Feelings," at the end of this chapter, to help students chart the feelings words they read, describe who felt it, what brought it on, and what actions followed.

- After creating an Inventory with the students, play a game called, "Can you find?" Provide clues to the pronunciation and meaning of the word. Ask: *Can you find a word that begins with the letter "m" and ends with the letter "d"? It tells how I would feel if someone took my lunch money.*

CLASSROOM CONNECTION

Ms. Vasquez is conducting a mini lesson during a reading-writing workshop. Her third-grade students are brainstorming what it feels like when someone hurts their feelings. **Embarrassing, sad, unfair,** and **angry** are some of their responses. Ms. Vasquez writes a list of these feelings on a piece of chart paper and hangs it in the room so everyone can see it. She reminds the students, "Remember that your journals are private. Here is a list of words that may help you write about feelings that you have as different situations happen at home and at school."

Ms. Vasquez recognizes that this activity has served its purpose many times throughout the year. For example, if Jenny hurt Caitlin's feelings, Ms. Vasquez would discreetly ask Jenny to silently read her journal entry describing what it felt like when her feelings were hurt. Ms. Vasquez states that the activity, "Made it easier for students to use their past experiences to empathize with their classmates. It became easier for students to realize how other students had actually been affected, and also made it easier for apologies to be offered and accepted."

Tool: Anger Thermometer and Anger Reducers

One of the most difficult emotions that students deal with is anger: it often erupts quickly and is difficult to control. It is important for students to recognize the things that trigger their anger, to understand the impact that anger has on conflict, and to develop strategies to manage their anger.

Assure students that anger is a natural emotion; it is a common response to an experience we find distressing. The Anger Thermometer uses the analogy of a thermometer to help them understand their levels of anger. Instead of temperature markings, the thermometer shows intensifying levels of anger. Students then identify the intensity of their angry feelings in certain situations, an awareness that can help them become more adept at applying appropriate strategies to manage those feelings.

Create an Anger Thermometer from tagboard or foam board. It is helpful, particularly for younger students, if it is large and can be physically manipulated. See the sample below. Use red yarn, or a red ribbon strung through slits at the bottom and top of the thermometer to represent mercury so the "mercury" can be manipulated easily. Label the side of the thermometer with the following words, starting with the first at the top:

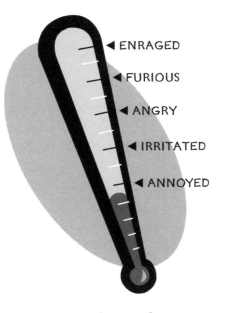

- Enraged

- Furious

- Angry

- Irritated

- Annoyed

To introduce the concept of the Anger Thermometer, share a short story that is relevant to the lives of the students and involves a character who becomes increasingly angry. It usually works best if a teacher who knows the students makes up the story. As the character gets more and more angry, call on volunteers to manipulate the "mercury" so that it rises as the anger level of the main character rises. A sample story might read like this:

Billy woke up, looked out the window, and realized that the sky was lighter than usual. He looked at his alarm clock and noticed that the alarm hadn't gone off. He would really have to hurry to get to school on time. He was **annoyed***. He ran to the bus stop just in time to see the back of the bus. It had already pulled away. Now he would have to ask his mother for a ride. She would not be happy. Billy was* **irritated** *and, as it turned out, so was his mother. She said that he would have to go to bed at 8:00 P.M. for a week. This was one hour earlier than his regular bedtime! Now, Billy was* **angry***. When Billy arrived at school, he explained the reason he was late for class. His teacher was understanding, but said that he would have to make up his work during recess. He wouldn't be able to play football, and he was the quarterback. His team was undefeated. Now, Billy was* **furious***. When his friends came back from recess, they announced that they had lost a game for the first time. They called him a "loser" and ignored him for the rest of* *the school day. After school, no one would sit with him on the bus ride home. Billy felt that he had been treated unfairly all day. Now he was* **enraged**.

Ask students questions that allow them to explore the concept of the thermometer:

1. How can being angry be like having a fever?
    - A fever can be measured in degrees from cool to very hot. Anger can be measured on the Anger Thermometer.
    - The higher your body temperature rises, the worse you feel. The higher you go on the Anger Thermometer, the angrier you are.

2. What do people who care for you do when you have a high temperature?
    - They try to cool you down with medicine, or a cold cloth, etc. These are called fever reducers.
    - They don't let you leave the house until your fever cools down.

3. What does this have to do with anger?
    - You should try to cool off and bring down your temperature on the Anger Thermometer before causing a conflict or dealing with conflict situations.

Next, give each student an Anger Thermometer handout. Describe four situations that could occur in the classroom, cafeteria, etc. Have students determine the level of anger that they would feel in each situation and color in the degree of anger that they would feel on the Anger Thermometer. Discuss how students felt. Ask them to brainstorm additional situations that make them angry. Record the brainstormed list. Label the chart, "Our Anger Triggers." Display the chart in the room.

Next, explore the idea of anger reducers. Anger reducers can help students calm down instead of reacting to situations while they are angry. Elicit ideas from the students by asking: *What are some healthy, productive ways to calm yourself down?* Some ideas for reducers include:

- **Ballooning** — Take a deep breath and blow yourself up like a balloon. Gradually let the air out. Breathe slowly until you are deflated.

- **Draining** — Tighten up every part of your body. Begin releasing the tension one body part at a time. Begin with your head, neck, arms, etc. Imagine that your anger is a pool of water now at the bottom of your feet — it has drained to the floor.

- **Self-talk** — Tell yourself that it's better to calm down than to "lose it." Look at the negative side of losing your temper, and choose not to do so.

- **Changing the channel** — Picture yourself in a peaceful setting, far away from the place you're in now. For example, lying on a sunny beach, or walking in the woods. This is a way to divert your thinking from the issue that is making you angry.

Record other ideas for anger reducers on chart paper. Ask students to look at all of the ideas and decide which might work for them. Keep the chart visible in the classroom as a reminder for students to try new techniques when they get angry. As an additional activity, ask students to draw four stick figures with voice balloons. Then ask them to illustrate four different ways they can handle anger.

Older students can commit to managing their feelings by filling out an Anger Agreement Contract; this helps them to formulate a plan for the next time they become angry. (See a sample at the end of this chapter.)

How to Use the Anger Thermometer and Anger Reducers Tool

- In literature the class is reading, identify the levels of anger that the characters are experiencing, either by examples from text or by inference. Look for ways that characters deal with their angry feelings and include them on the class list.

- When a character's angry feelings prove to be destructive, discuss the alternatives that the character might have chosen. How might she have reduced her anger and how might this have helped the character get along with others?

- Use the vocabulary you have taught students about anger when discussing the characters in a story. For example, ask, "What *triggered* Moira's angry response?" and "What *reducers* could she have used?"

Tool: Role-Play

Role-plays are similar to skits; they simulate specific situations for the purpose of learning new skills or exploring new ways of relating together. Performing role-plays can help students explore feelings more deeply, become more comfortable using newly learned skills, and prepare them for similar situations in real life. Helpful guidelines for role-plays are:

- A character's name should not be the name of anyone in the class.

- No offensive language.

- No touching; that should include any type of "pretend" fighting.

Having students observe a good role-play can be very helpful, and lessens the "silliness" that students can do in role-playing. Invite another adult to role-play with you before you begin with students. Students like to see adult acting; it helps them to understand that developing a plot is important in role-playing.

One way to get students comfortable and used to performing in front of others is to begin with pantomiming. Explain that students are going to have an opportunity to be actors and actresses. Have them select a word from the Feelings Inventory and pantomime the word. The rest of the class should guess what word the student is acting out. Discuss with students how body language often indicates how someone is feeling. With older students, discuss how people can misread emotions.

How to Use the Role-Play Tool

- Each time new words are added to the class Feelings Inventory, repeat the pantomiming activity described above.

- Choose scenes from literature that the class is reading and ask groups of students to role-play the events that occur, paying particular attention to the feelings that the characters are experiencing.

- Ask students to predict the outcome of a story by using the feelings they have observed so far in a story. In groups, ask students to role-play possible endings for the story.

- Identify situations in which students often hurt the feelings of others, and assign groups scenarios to role-play that explore ways to deal productively with hurt feelings.

LINKS TO LITERATURE

When Sophie Gets Angry...Really, Really Angry

Molly Bang

New York: Scholastic Paperbacks, 2004 • Grade Level: K-2

Sophie is so angry that she is ready to explode. When her sister grabs a toy that Sophie must share with her, Sophie falls over a toy truck. Sophie handles her anger by running and crying, and then retreating into nature until she is calm enough to go home. Sophie is welcomed back when she returns home.

 Feelings Inventory Tool: This is a good book to use for discussing the concept of anger as a secondary emotion. Help students to recognize what might be the initial feeling that then becomes the feeling of anger. That is, one may first feel hurt, and then become angry; or embarrassed and then angry; sad and then angry, and so on. Ask students to determine what initial feelings Sophie might have felt before she showed her anger.

 Anger Thermometer and Anger Reducers Tool: Ask students to identify the actions that made Sophie angry, and determine where her anger was on the Anger Thermometer. What feelings besides anger might she feel in these moments? Discuss what anger reducers she used to calm down. Ask students to discuss a time when they were really, really angry, like Sophie, and what they did to calm themselves down. Discuss the strategies that Sophie used to calm down. Then ask students to illustrate a healthy reducer that they might try and title the illustration "When I am really, really angry I will _____."

 Role-Play Tool: Ask students to choose a time when they became angry and then managed their anger, and have them create a brief scene that illustrates that time to share with the class.

How Are You Peeling? Foods with Moods

Saxton Freymann and Joost Elffers

New York: Scholastic Paperbacks, 2004 • Grade Level: K-3

This book provides an entertaining format for building a feelings vocabulary and exploring the idea that the same situations can evoke a range of emotions for different individuals. The fruits and vegetables begin by asking the reader, "How are you peeling?" Emotions and illustrations are then linked to situations common in students' everyday lives, as well as their reactions to these situations.

Feelings Inventory Tool: After adding any new words from this book to the Feelings Inventory the class has created, create a Feelings Wheel based on these words. To do so, divide a large circle of colored tagboard into at least eight sections that resemble pieces of a pie. In each section, place cut-outs of fruits and vegetables that represent different emotions from the book, one emotion per section. Have students make figures of themselves out of clothespins decorated with yarn and fabric. When students enter the classroom in the morning, have them hook their clothespins next to the fruit or vegetable on the wheel that represents how they are feeling. This provides you with a general idea of the emotional climate of the day. During a class meeting or Gathering, students can discuss why they have chosen that emotion. For an alternative, provide a variety of cups labeled with different feelings words. As each student enters the classroom, he places a tongue depressor with his name on it into one of the cups that reflects how he is feeling at the time.

Anger Thermometer Tool: Refer to the Anger Thermometer to see if any of the feelings words from the story appear on the thermometer the class has been working with. If the students notice additional words that they would like to add, discuss where they might fit on the thermometer.

 Role-Play Tool: Play the pantomime game with the new words. Older students can explore possible miscommunication that body language can lead to.

Best Friends

Steven Kellogg

New York: Puffin Books, 1992 • Grade Level: K-3

Kathy and Louise are inseparable until Louise's aunt and uncle arrive to take Louise camping for the summer. Prior to Louise's adventurous trip, the two girls did everything together, and while Louise is away, her friend Kathy continually feels lonely and sorry for herself. When Kathy receives a post card from her friend informing her about the fun she is having and the new friends she is making, Kathy becomes extremely jealous. Kathy is hesitant and acts rather strangely upon Louise's return. A surprise ending helps Kathy realize that she is loved and valued by her best friend after all.

 Feelings Inventory Tool: Ask students to write about a friend that they have and to include words that describe how the friend makes them feel. Add these words to the class feelings inventory.

 Anger Thermometer and Anger Reducers Tool: Ask students to choose a scene and chart the intensity of feelings they see on the thermometer. Identify whether the characters used reducers and if they were effective. If not, brainstorm ideas for techniques that might have been used.

 Role-Play Tool: In groups, ask students to talk about an experience they have had that is similar to that of Kathy and Louise and how it made them feel. Have each group choose an incident to perform for the class.

Love That Dog

Sharon Creech

New York: HarperTrophy, 2003 • Grade Level: 3+

At first, Jack doesn't want to write poetry for his teacher because he thinks that it's something only girls write. Eventually, he finds his voice as a poet, and writes about his love for his dog and the grief he experiences after the dog's death.

 Feelings Inventory Tool: Create an inventory for this book, or add the feelings to the class inventory. Ask students to talk about a favorite pet of their own, and to describe the emotions they feel for that pet.

Anger Thermometer and Anger Reducers Tool: Ask students to label the feelings on the Thermometer handout with the feelings that Jack experiences in this story. Next to each feeling, ask students to write the incident that leads Jack to express this feeling. Ask students to list ways Jack manages his strong emotions.

 Role-Play Tool: Ask groups of students to choose an incident from the story to perform, paying particular attention to the feelings they think that Jack is experiencing. The class can then try to guess which feelings they're observing in the role-play.

Words of Stone

Kevin Henkes

New York: HarperTrophy, 2005　•　Grade Level: 3+

Words of Stone is the story of Blaze and Joselle, two troubled students who face many challenges, including their new friendship. Blaze, still coping with his mother's death, invents imaginary friends. Each year, the imaginary friend is unable to fulfill Blaze's needs and he buries his friend on top of a hill, marking his grave with a stone. Joselle, abandoned by her mother, who is supposedly traveling across the country with her new boyfriend, is so miserable that she wants to know that someone else's life is worse than hers. When she finds out about Blaze's secret, she rearranges Blaze's stone graves to spell Rena, the name of his deceased mother. Joselle wasn't bargaining for the fact that she and Blaze, two very different students, would become friends. Both students feel mixed emotions about one another and the conditions of their lives.

 Feelings Inventory Tool: Have students identify the different feelings Joselle and Blaze feel throughout the story and add them to the Feelings Inventory. They can also explore the feelings in the text using the Finding the Feelings handout at the end of this chapter.

 Anger Thermometer and Anger Reducer Tool: Choose a scene from the book and ask students to create a thermometer and label the emotions that the characters experience. Then, have them identify any reducers the characters used and discuss whether or not they were effective.

 Role-Play Tool: Ask students to create role-plays of scenes from the story, paying particular attention to portraying the feelings of the characters.

Angry Dragon

Thierry Robberecht

New York: Clarion, 2004
Grade Level: K-1

A boy describes how his anger turns him into a dragon, and how he feels. He ends up crying so hard that his tears put out the fire. He is a little boy again, and his parents assure him they still love him.

The Grouchy Ladybug

Eric Carle

New York: HarperCollins, 1999
Grade Level: K-1

A grouchy ladybug, looking for a fight, challenges everyone she meets, regardless of their size. She finally learns good manners and how to respect others.

Sometimes I'm Bombaloo

Rachel Vail

New York: Scholastic, 2005
Grade Level: K-1

Katie Honors tells how she usually behaves, how she acts when she lets her anger get away, and how she then gets back to normal.

Oliver Button is a Sissy

Tomie de Paola

Orlando, FL: Voyager Books, 1990
Grade Level: K-2

Oliver becomes a target of teasing because he prefers dancing to football. He rises above the taunts by doing what he does best and being recognized for his talent.

A Bad Case of Stripes

David Shannon

New York: Scholastic Paperbacks, 2004
Grade Level: K-2

Camilla Cream worries too much about what others think of her and tries desperately to please everyone. She's cured when she learns to relax and accept herself.

A to Z: Do You Ever Feel Like Me?: A Guessing Alphabet of Feelings, Words, and Other Cool Stuff

Bonnie Hausman

Photographs by Sandi Fellman
New York: Dutton, 1999
Grade Level: K-2

A clever list of situations describes feelings that the reader must guess.

Peaceful Piggy Meditation

Kerry Lee MacLean

Morton Grove, IL: Whitman, 2004
Grade Level: K-3

A group of pigs show how to calm down in the midst of anxiety, stress, or anger.

Lizzy's Ups and Downs: Not an Ordinary School Day

Jessica Harper

New York: HarperCollins, 2004
Grade Level: K-3

After a day in school, Lizzy finds satisfaction in listing for her mother all the feelings she has had during the day.

Mrs. Biddlebox

Linda Smith

New York: HarperCollins, 2002
Grade Level: 1-3

Mrs. Biddlebox wraps up a gloomy day, bakes it, and eats it.

Dear Mr. Henshaw

Beverly Cleary

New York: HarperTrophy
Grade Level: 4+

A boy's personal letters and private diary show his feelings about his parents' divorce and his growth in maturity.

NAME _____ DATE _____

Feelings Inventory

absorbed
engrossed
involved

affectionate
appreciative
friendly
helpful
loving
tender

afraid
alarmed
anxious
apprehensive
concerned
dreading
fearful
frightened
scared
startled
terrified
worried

alive
amazed
animated
astonished
breathless
buoyant
dazzled
eager
ecstatic
elated

electrified
energetic
enlivened

aloof
cold
distant
detached
withdrawn

amused
tickled
pleased

angry
aggravated
annoyed
cross
disgruntled
edgy
exasperated
frustrated
furious
hot
indignant
infuriated
irate
irked
irritated
mad
vexed

apathetic
bored
uninterested
dull
humdrum
indifferent
anguished
grief stricken
brokenhearted
hurt
disappointed
chagrined
embarrassed
guilty

averse
disliking
hating
hostile
appalled
disgusted
dismayed
revolted
horrified
repelled
shocked

beat
breathless
exhausted
fatigued
listless
tired

weary
worn out

bitter
embittered
rancorous
resentful
sour

bewildered
confused
perplexed

blissful
expansive
glorious
glowing
grateful
inspired
moved
radiant
rapturous
spellbound

calm
contented
mellow
peaceful
quiet
relaxed
restored
serene
still
tranquil

Feelings Inventory
continued

carefree
cheerful
delighted
glad
gleeful
good-humored
happy
joyful
merry

comfortable
cozy
cushy

confident
proud
secure
relieved

curious
inquisitive
interested
intrigued

dejected
depressed
despairing
despondent
discouraged
disheartened

downcast
downhearted
gloomy
heavy
melancholic
miserable
sorrowful
unnerved

despairing
pessimistic

diffident
doubtful
hesitant
reluctant
uncertain

displeased
sad
unhappy
woeful

encouraged
expectant
hopeful
optimistic

enthusiastic
exalted
excited
exhilarated
exuberant
fascinated
invigorated
jubilant
keyed-up
overjoyed
stimulated
thrilled

envious
jealous

exposed
insecure
sensitive
shaky
unsteady
vulnerable

fidgety
impatient
irritable
jittery
nervous
restless
tense
uptight

forlorn
lonely

fulfilled
gratified
satisfied

refreshed
reinvigorated
renewed
revived

suspicious
distrustful

thankful
touched
grateful

uncomfortable
uneasy

upset
agitated
disquieted
distressed
distraught
disturbed
troubled

Finding the Feelings

Directions: As you read, find as many feelings words as possible. Fill out the chart.

Feeling Word	Who Felt It	What Brought It On	What Actions Followed

Anger Thermometer

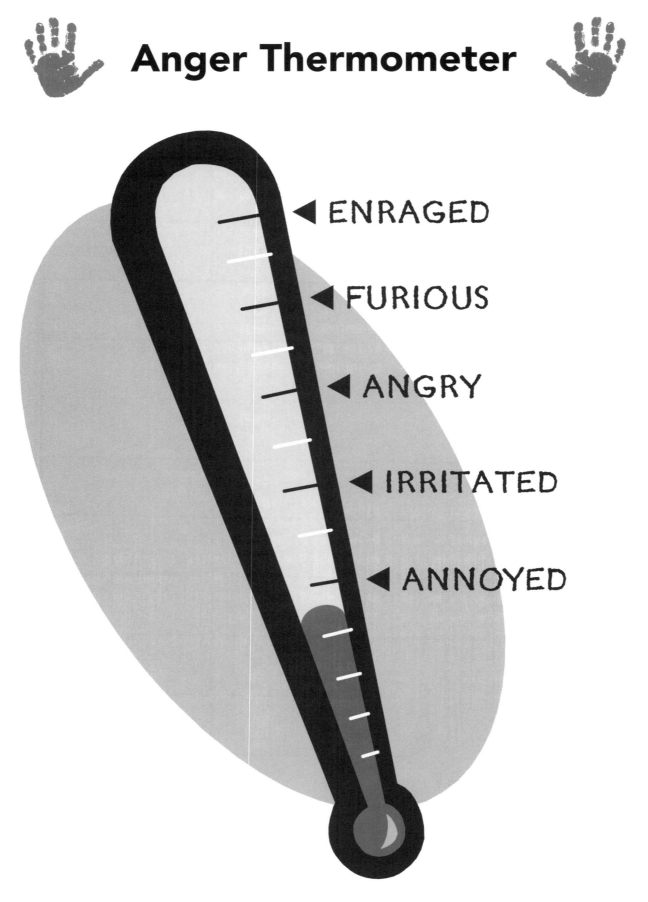

◀ ENRAGED

◀ FURIOUS

◀ ANGRY

◀ IRRITATED

◀ ANNOYED

NAME _____ DATE _____

Anger Agreement

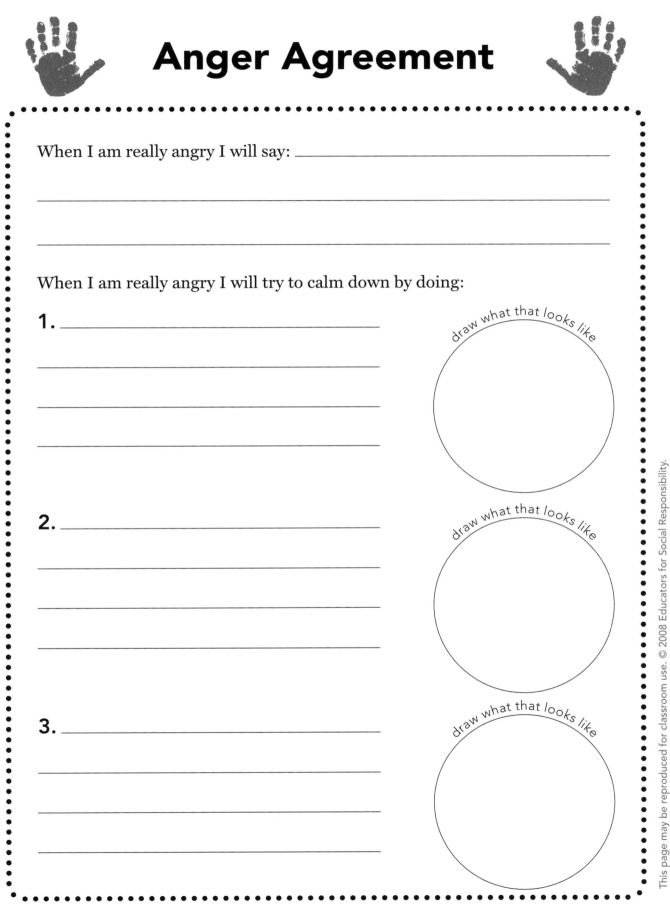

When I am really angry I will say: _____

_____

_____

When I am really angry I will try to calm down by doing:

1. _____

_____

_____

_____

draw what that looks like

2. _____

_____

_____

_____

draw what that looks like

3. _____

_____

_____

_____

draw what that looks like

Chapter 3

Conflict Management
and Decision Making

Managing conflict is an essential part of a productive and caring classroom. Despite the fact that it is often perceived as negative because of the difficulties it can cause, conflict is a normal and natural part of everyone's life. If students have the opportunity to talk about conflict, however, and are given some tools to deal with it, conflict can feel much more manageable.

For many young people, conflicts can get out of control very quickly, and when conflicts escalate, they increase in intensity. Conflicts escalate because of the actions of the people involved, but recognizing that this escalation is happening can be difficult since emotions usually become strong. The most difficult time to deal with a conflict is when it has already escalated to its height. People are most angry at this point, most polarized in their positions, and least likely to want to try to work anything out. Working with students to explore the concept of conflict escalation as well as the tools for de-escalating it can teach them ways to slow this rapid ascent.

Unfortunately, many students view conflict as a win or lose experience. While conflicts can end with a win-lose situation, in which one person gets what she wants and the other doesn't, or a lose-lose situation, in which neither party gets what she wants, conflicts can also result in a win-win solution. When win-win solutions are achieved, all disputants get what they want or need. Students should be encouraged to do two things: approach conflict from a win-win perspective, and work with others to achieve win-win solutions.

Students can respond to conflict in many different ways. With a repertoire of different techniques, they will be able to choose the appropriate response. Exploring six conflict styles will help to build this repertoire.

Students acquire conflict resolution skills in two ways. One is to learn a specific strategy that helps resolve a particular kind of issue. Flipping a coin and "rock, paper, scissors" are two examples of useful strategies. The other way is through open-ended problem solving. The ABCD Problem Solving Tool is an easy way for students to remember a format for problem solving. ABCD problem solving involves identifying the problem you are trying to solve, coming up with possible ideas for solving it, choosing the solution that is most likely to get what you want, and implementing the solution.

This chapter presents tools to help students identify conflict situations, learn to approach a conflict from a win-win perspective, develop a repertoire of techniques for dealing with conflict, and engage in active problem solving. These tools are:

- The Conflict Escalator and De-escalation

- Win-Win Grid

- Understanding Conflict Styles

- ABCD Problem Solving

Tool: The Conflict Escalator and De-escalation

When conflict intensifies or gets worse, we say it escalates. Escalation means that the disputants become angrier, and their positions become more polarized. Most conflicts escalate in a step-by-step manner, like going up the steps of an escalator, with each person's actions leading to a response that makes the conflict worse. For many students, however, conflict may escalate so fast it feels as if they are riding an express elevator. Once the conflict starts, it escalates immediately to its height. In fact, many students don't even recognize that they are in a conflict until it has reached its top. Unfortunately, the more quickly the conflict has escalated, the more difficult it is to de-escalate it and resolve it. Examining the concept of conflict escalation helps students do three things:

- recognize that a conflict has begun and is escalating

- identify points to try to de-escalate the conflict

- see how different behaviors may make the conflict get better or worse

There are a number of ways to introduce escalation to students. Providing a graphic and explaining the stair-step pattern is a helpful way to begin.

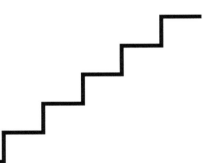

Explain that each step on the escalator represents a behavior or an action that makes the conflict worse. A conflict might begin when someone says or does something that we find upsetting. Then, because we're upset, we say or do something in response that upsets the other person, who then becomes upset and says or does something upsetting to us, and then we're ascending the escalator!

Doing role-plays can help students to explore this concept further. Choose scenarios that often occur in school settings, such as cutting in line, unkind personal comments made by one student to another, or difficulties working in groups caused by others not meeting deadlines. Be sure to set clear ground rules for role-plays — using names other than real ones, no bad language, and no touching are basic to most role-playing. At the conclusion of the role-play, chart responses in two columns: *What Escalates?* and *What De-escalates?* De-escalating behaviors or actions are those that make the situation calmer and help move it toward a peaceful solution.

An alternative way to introduce escalation and de-escalation is to read a short picture book and have students identify escalating behaviors. A great story for this is "The Zax," by Dr. Seuss, from *The Sneetches and Other Stories* (1961, Geisel and Geisel). Before you begin reading, ask the students to listen to the story, and when they hear something that might escalate the situation to say, "Uh-oh!" (Note: If you want to save the ending of the story to explore the win-win approach, which is the next tool in this chapter, stop before the last page.) Ask students which behaviors escalated the conflict and chart these as escalators. Ask what each character could have done to de-escalate (they don't!) and chart these possibilities as de-escalators.

De-escalators can be a variety of ideas, such as softening one's tone of voice, apologizing, or listening to the other person's point of view. Older students will see that some of the same words can be placed on both the escalating side of the chart and on the de-escalating side, depending on how they're used. Humor, for example, can be cruel and demeaning, and be an escalator, but it can also be a diversion that makes both people laugh.

Imagine travelers at an airport, getting on the escalator with their baggage. Some carry small bags and others very large ones. Older students can explore the additional concept of baggage — feelings or thoughts we carry with us into conflict situations, such as how we feel at the time, including our emotions and our state of health, our previous experiences with the person, how capable we feel about dealing with the conflict, and our cultural norms (some cultures label certain behaviors "disrespectful," but the same behaviors may be considered acceptable in other cultures). All of this baggage can cause us to skip the bottom "step" of the escalator at the beginning of a conflict and start midway, or near the top. Emotional baggage can cause us to react quickly, and sometimes inappropriately, making it hard for others to understand our motivation or our actions.

How to Use the Conflict Escalator and De-escalation Tool

- Many books have a clearly defined sequence of escalating behaviors. Ask students to chart behaviors that intensify conflict on a conflict escalator. (See the end of this chapter for a format.) Above each step, students should write the action/behavior that escalates the situation, and below each step, a feeling word that would describe how the receiver might feel about this behavior. This visual tool helps students see that *feelings* drive escalation.

- Use the vocabulary of *escalating* and *de-escalating* when students are involved in conflicts with each other. Instead of placing blame, ask what escalated the conflict and if anyone did anything to de-escalate it. Work with students to develop a large repertoire of de-escalating behaviors. Some of these might be using anger management tools, or being assertive instead of aggressive or passive.

- Use the worksheet *Escalating and De-escalating Behaviors — What's Helpful? What's Risky?* at the end of this chapter to help students identify behaviors and outcomes in pieces of literature.

- Provide the students with a copy of a conflict escalator from the end of the chapter. Ask them to think about a recent conflict they had, and ask them to chart the conflict on the escalator. As part of their illustrations, ask them to represent the baggage they brought to this conflict.

Tool: Win–Win Grid

Explain that several different outcomes are possible when people are in a conflict: win-lose, lose-lose, and win-win. Win-win occurs when the needs of both people are met. In lose-lose, neither person's needs are met, and in win-lose one person's needs are met and the other's are not.

Read "The Zax" to students, stopping before the end. Ask students to predict four possible endings for the story. Write the predictions in a win-win grid like the one below. Then read the last page, and ask which outcome Dr. Seuss used. Ask students to think about a time when they experienced a lose-lose outcome. Very often, students have experiences that can be labeled as lose-lose even when they first felt that they had "won."

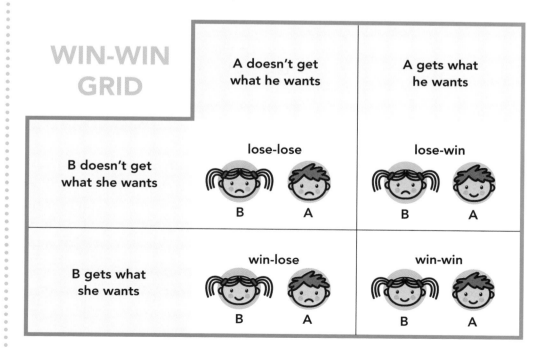

- Ask students to think about a conflict they have had and determine whether its outcome was win-lose, lose-lose, or win-win. Organize them in pairs, and have them take turns sharing the conflict and its outcome.

- Use the win-win grid vocabulary to explore the outcome of a story. For example, at the conclusion of a story, ask students to categorize the ending into one of the types of solutions represented in the grid.

- Before the conclusion of a story that the class is reading, ask groups to role-play possible outcomes, ending with a win-win solution.

Tool: Understanding Conflict Styles

Explain that there are many ways, or styles, of responding to conflict situations. However, sometimes people get stuck in one particular way and sometimes that way, or style, may not be the most helpful one for resolving a particular conflict. Therefore, it's helpful to understand the styles we already use and add other styles to our repertoire that we can use depending on the situation.

A number of surveys that students can complete are available to help them determine which style they use most often (http://peace.mennolink.org/resources/conflictyouth/quiz.html provides surveys that are age-appropriate). The survey at the end of this chapter can be used with older students. Students should fill it out individually and be as honest as possible. Allow them to keep the results confidential.

If you choose not to use the survey, review the six styles by listing them on chart paper or on the board, or by distributing the handout at the end of this chapter. Alternative style titles have been provided here for use with younger students.

Briefly explain each of the styles. It might be helpful to write the words in quotation marks to serve as reminders for the latter part of the activity.

- Directing/Controlling *(Alternative: Getting Our Way)*
  "My way or the highway." We do not, cannot, or will not bargain or give in. At times we are standing up for rights or beliefs that are important to us. We can also be pursuing what we want at the expense of others, or be unable to see a way to negotiate to get what we want.

- Collaborating *(Alternative: Working It Out)*
  "Let's sit down and work this out." We work with others to find a way to get all of our needs met. We see the other people as partners, and spend time to find solutions to our conflict.

- Compromising *(Alternative: Making a Deal)*
  "Let's both give a little" or "Something is better than nothing." Each party gives up something for a solution that may only meet some of our needs.

- Accommodating *(Alternative: Giving In)*
  "Whatever you want is fine" or "It doesn't matter anyway." We yield to another, and meet another's needs but not our own. We may do this to keep a good relationship or to get our way another time.

- Avoiding/Denying *(Alternative: Running Away)*
  "Let's skip it" or "Problem? I don't see a problem." We don't deal with the conflict, or we act as if the conflict isn't happening. We may leave others to deal with it.

- Appealing to a Greater Authority or Third Party
  (Alternative: Getting Help)
  "Help me out here." We turn to others who may have more authority, influence, or skills in dealing with the conflict.

After students become familiar with the different styles, divide them into groups. Assign a style to each group and have them create a role-play that illustrates that style. Have each group perform their role-play. The rest of the class should try to guess which style is being illustrated.

An additional activity that enables older students to explore this in more depth is to identify potential uses and limitations of each style. Have students work in groups to complete the following chart:

Name of Style	When/in which situations is this style helpful?	When/in which situations is this style not useful or helpful?

Review the answers in a class discussion, and post the charts as visual reminders for students.

How to Use the Conflict Styles Tool

- When students experience conflict with others, ask what style they have tried, and what other styles might be helpful.

- Use the handout "Conflict Styles in Literature" that follows this chapter to explore a text or excerpt.

- When characters in literature get stuck in a style that is not useful or helpful to the situation, brainstorm other styles with the students that the character could have tried.

Tool: ABCD Problem Solving

Sometimes students have never thought about how normal and natural conflict is. Once they understand this, let them know that it's helpful to have a format to use when people want to work out a problem and achieve a win-win solution. Sometimes it is necessary to spend time exploring possibilities in order to get to a good resolution for a problem. Review the format for this tool:

A Ask what the problem is.

B Brainstorm solutions to the problem.

C Choose one of the solutions offered.

D Do it!

When people are willing to problem solve, they will often find many ways to get to a win-win situation. This tool helps students manage the process and provides alternatives if the first solution doesn't work out.

A useful way to introduce this tool is to read a selection from a book in which characters are involved in a conflict, but to stop before they come to a resolution. Have the class apply the ABCD Problem Solving Tool to the problem in the story. Examine the actual outcome of the conflict and determine whether that resolution is a win-win solution.

Ask students to think about conflicts they have had and to use this tool to think of possible resolutions that may not have occurred to them before.

How to Use the ABCD Problem Solving Tool

- When students come to you for help in solving a problem, encourage them use this tool to solve the problem themselves.

- Characters in many books get stuck when they try to work problems out. Use this tool with students to explore possible resolutions to conflicts in literature.

- When characters come up with a solution that doesn't work, ask students to use this tool and rewrite the outcome of the story.

LINKS TO
LITERATURE

Owen

Kevin Henkes

New York: Greenwillow Books, 1993   •   Grade level: K-3

Owen has a yellow blanket that he takes with him wherever he goes. "Fuzzy goes where I go," says Owen, but his neighbor, Mrs. Tweezers, disagrees. Owen's parents are worried because he is going to kindergarten and they wonder if Mrs. Tweezers is right. After trying various ways to separate Owen from his blanket, Owen's mother comes up with a solution that everyone is pleased with.

 Conflict Escalator and De-escalation Tool: As you read aloud to students, ask them to identify escalating and de-escalating behaviors. They can either say "Uh-oh" or show thumbs up to identify escalation, and show thumbs down for de-escalation.

 Win-Win Grid Tool: Stop reading at the climax of the story and ask students to chart possible outcomes using the win-win grid. They can work in pairs or groups and should be ready to justify their responses.

 Conflict Styles Tool: Ask students to identify which character uses which style when dealing with other people and when trying to solve the yellow blanket problem.

 ABCD Problem Solving Tool: Just before reading the end of the story, ask students to use the ABCD Problem Solving tool to problem solve the blanket issue. Have them discuss it orally with you, or in small groups that report to the class.

It's Mine!

Leo Lionni

New York: Dragonfly Books, 1996 • Grade Level: K-3

It's Mine tells the story of three frogs, Lydia, Milton, and Robert, who inhabit the same pond and are unable to share their resources. It takes a severe thunderstorm and the help of a friend to help the three do some problem solving. They all enjoy the peacefulness that results when they end their bickering and stop competing.

 Conflict Escalator and De-Escalation Tool: Ask students to identify escalating behaviors that they see in the interaction among the three frogs. They can either say "Uh-oh" or show thumbs up to identify escalation, and thumbs down for de-escalation.

 Win-Win Grid: Stop reading before the end of the book and ask students to complete a win-win grid charting possible outcomes.

 Conflict Styles Tool: Identify which conflict styles each of the three frogs uses. Determine which are helpful in the situation and which are not.

 ABCD Problem Solving Tool: Just before reading the end, ask students to use the ABCD Problem Solving tool, either orally, with you, or in small groups that report to the class.

Angel Child, Dragon Child

Michele Maria Surat

New York: Scholastic Paperbacks, 1989 • Grade level: K-3

This book tells the story of Ut, her father, and her siblings, who are from Vietnam. They experience many difficulties adjusting to school in the U.S. because a group of students, led by Raymond, the "red-headed boy," make fun of their language, clothes, and customs. Ut sometimes has to be a brave, fierce Dragon Child when she meets with the challenges of a new language or teasing. But she wants to be a happy Angel Child. When she and Raymond end up in the principal's office, the principal requires Raymond to listen to Ut's story and write it down. As a result, Raymond and Ut come to see and appreciate each other through new eyes. The students decide to hold a fund-raising fair in order to bring Ut's mother from Vietnam to be reunited with her family.

 Conflict Escalator and De-Escalation Tool: In groups, ask students to chart escalating and de-escalating behaviors that they find in the story. When the characters do or say something that they think is escalating, they should draw the step going up. If there are any words or actions that de-escalate the conflict, they should draw the step going down. Older students can write down the feelings associated with each escalating and de-escalating situation under the appropriate step.

 Win-Win Grid Tool: Using a win-win grid, ask students to brainstorm possible endings for the story. Stop reading at certain points, and ask students to predict possible outcomes.

 Conflict Styles Tool: Ut uses a number of conflict styles throughout the story. Ask students to identify the styles and to determine whether or not they were helpful in the situation.

ABCD Problem Solving Tool: Divide students into groups of three. Ask them to play the roles of the principal, Ut, and Raymond, and show what an ABCD Problem-Solving process would look like.

The Well: David's Story

Mildred D. Taylor

New York: Dial Books for Young Readers, 1995   •   Grade Level: 4+

The Well, by Mildred Taylor, is a prequel to *Roll of Thunder, Hear My Cry.* It is set in the South during a time when daily life is dominated by white men's rules. The Logans, a black family, are landowners living among white neighbors, many of whom are sharecroppers. One of the sharecropper families, the Simms, is particularly resentful of the Logan's prosperity, and an ongoing feud exists between the two families. When the story begins, the characters are coping with a drought. The Logans' well provides the only source of water in the area. Mama Logan shares her water with everyone, black and white alike. Her son, Hammer, cannot understand how Mama can share with the Simms, who have been particularly cruel to his family. Hammer is especially resentful of Charlie Simms, who degrades Hammer for being black.

Conflict Escalator and De-Escalation Tool: Divide students into small groups. Provide different excerpts to each group and have them chart escalating and de-escalating behaviors. Under each step, ask students to write the character's feelings associated with the behavior. Ask what baggage the characters bring to the situation, such as prejudice or anger.

You can also use the worksheet *Escalating and De-escalating Behaviors — What's Helpful? What's Risky?* at the end of this chapter to help students identify behaviors and outcomes.

Win-Win Grid Tool: Ask students to predict possible outcomes of the story at various stopping points. They should use the win-win grid to make their predictions. Discuss what decisions the characters actually made.

Conflict Styles Tool: Divide students into small groups. Ask them to complete the "Conflict Styles in Literature" handout for a particular excerpt.

ABCD Problem Solving Tool: Divide students into small groups and assign each group a scenario from the book. Have students role-play the scenario using ABCD problem solving to resolve the issues the characters face.

Matthew and Tilly

Rebecca C. Jones

New York: Puffin Books, 1995
Grade Level: K-3

Matthew and Tilly are close friends who live in the inner city. They play and work together every day. Problems begin when they argue over a broken crayon and go their separate ways. The children soon discover that many of their favorite games aren't as much fun to play alone. They make up and play together again.

King of the Playground

Phyllis Reynolds Naylor

New York: Aladdin Paperbacks, 1994
Grade Level: K-3

Kevin goes to the playground every day, only to be ousted by Sammy's threats. Kevin's dad mildly points out that Sammy's fierce notions are impractical and unlikely, and helps Kevin realize that he's not helpless. Finally, Kevin gets up his courage and counters Sammy's threats with an imaginative—and logical—verbal exchange. Then, the two settle down to play in the sandbox together.

Chachaji's Cup

Uma Krishnaswami

San Francisco, CA: Children's Book Press, 2003
Grade Level: K-3

Neel tells of his storytelling uncle Chachaji, who always drinks tea from the cup his mother carried from Pakistan in 1947, the time of the partition of India. Neel accidentally breaks the cup, but finds a way that it can still hold memories.

Island of the Skog

Steven Kellogg

Penguin Young Readers Group, 1993
Grade Level: K-3

Jenny and her city-mouse friends set sail in search of a more peaceful place to live. They arrive on an island inhabited by a seemingly hostile Skog, with seemingly gigantic feet. But when the two parties finally meet face to face, they find they have a lot in common.

Hooway for Wodney Wat

Helen Lester

New York: Scholastic, 2006, 1999
Grade Level: K-3

Rodney Rat is teased unmercifully because he cannot pronounce his *r*'s. Then Camilla Capybara, a bully, joins the class and Rodney regains control for the class.

The Recess Queen

Alexis O'Neill

New York: Scholastic Press, 2002
Grade Level: K-4

Mean Jean is the reigning Recess Queen, and no one dares touch a ball, swing a bat, or use a slide until she says so. One day a puny new girl shows up and catches Mean Jean completely offguard by making her an offer she finds hard to refuse – an invitation to play. Soon they are best friends, and the playground is safe for all.

Say Something

Peggy Moss

Gardiner, ME: Tilbury House, 2004
Grade Level: K-5

A middle-school girl tells about a boy who always gets picked on, another who gets called names, and a girl who always sits by herself on the bus. When the narrator sits alone in the cafeteria because her friends are gone, she is taunted until she cries. Although the students at another table seem to feel sorry for her, no one says anything, and the narrator realizes what she needs to do. Later, she sits by the girl on the bus.

The Day I Saw My Father Cry

Bill Cosby

New York: Scholastic, 2000
Grade Level: 1-4

When Alan Mills died, Little Bill's dad cried. Alan had taught Little Bill and his brother Bobby to say, "Merry Christmas!" to de-escalate fights.

The War between the Vowels and the Consonants

Priscilla Turner

New York: Farrar Straus Giroux, 1999
Grade Level: 2-4

War escalates until the two groups of letters unite against the common enemy, a senseless scrawl. They go on to create all forms of literature.

The Cats in Krasinski Square

Karen Hesse

New York: Scholastic, 2004
Grade Level: 3-5

During the early 1940s in Nazi-occupied Poland, the young narrator passes as a Polish girl. She and her older sister Mira smuggle food to people in the Warsaw Ghetto. They hear that the Gestapo plan to take dogs and stop the passengers on a certain train from smuggling more food. So the locals gather up homeless cats and create chaos, allowing food distribution to continue.

Going Up the Conflict Escalator

The higher you go on the escalator, the harder it is to come back down.

Every step up the conflict escalator has feelings that go with it. As the conflict escalates, feelings intensify.

Behavior that makes the conflict worse will take the conflict up another step.

Everything you say or do is either a step up or a step down the conflict escalator

⭐ Nobody gets on the escalator empty handed. We bring baggage that can be filled with:

- past relationships

- current mood/feelings

- current feelings about the person

- assumptions and biases

- current feelings about conflict

- dominant communications and conflict styles

Escalating and De-escalating Behaviors
What's Helpful? What's Risky?

Directions: As you read a story, pay attention to characters' behaviors that impact the conflict. In the first chart, list the behaviors that make the conflict escalate. In the second chart, list how the characters make the conflict de-escalate. Write how you think each action, statement, or behavior is helpful or risky.

Character	Statement, action or behavior that escalates the conflict	How might it be helpful or useful?	How might it be risky or dangerous?

Character	Statement, action or behavior that de-escalates the conflict	How might it be helpful or useful?	How might it be risky or dangerous?

The Conflict Escalator

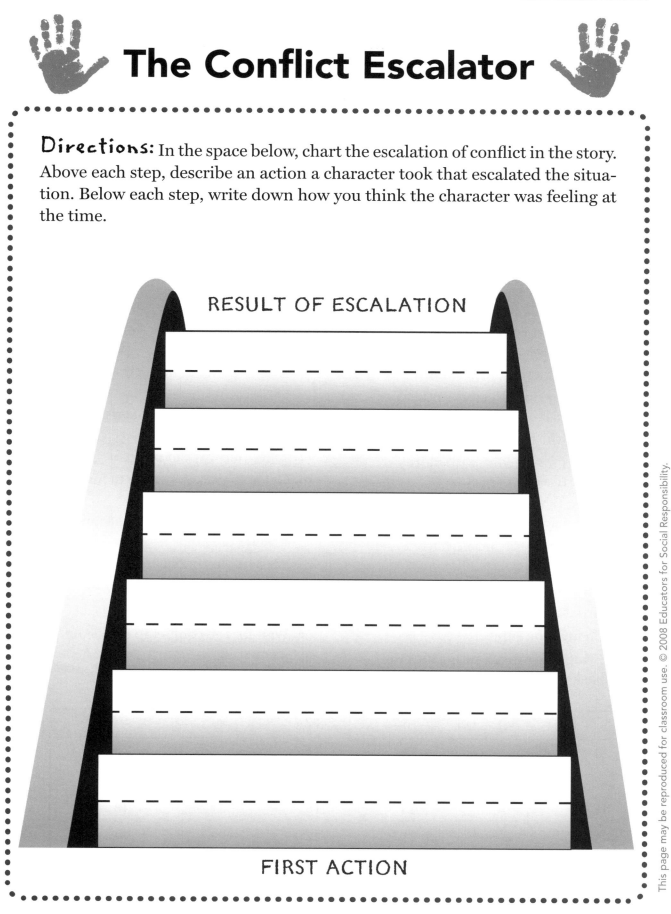

Directions: In the space below, chart the escalation of conflict in the story. Above each step, describe an action a character took that escalated the situation. Below each step, write down how you think the character was feeling at the time.

RESULT OF ESCALATION

FIRST ACTION

Conflict Management Styles Survey

Directions: Read each of the approaches listed and decide whether you use that response frequently, occasionally, or rarely during conflicts and disagreements. If it describes a frequent response, write "3" in the appropriate blank below. If it is an occasional response, write "2" in the blank. Write a "1" if you rarely use the response described.

How do you usually handle conflict?

1. Use all your resources to win
2. Try to deal with the other person's point of view
3. Look for a middle ground
4. Look for ways to let the other person win
5. Avoid the person
6. Look for someone with more expertise or experience
7. Insist that the other person do it your way
8. Investigate the problem from many angles
9. Try to reach a compromise
10. Give in
11. Change the subject
12. Bring in stronger authorities to back you up
13. Persevere until you get your way
14. Try to get all concerns out in the open
15. Give in a little; encourage the other party to do the same
16. Make quick agreements if only to keep the peace
17. Joke your way out of it
18. Get help from someone to make the decision
19. Decide what must be done and do it yourself
20. Present alternative to consider
21. Settle for a partial victory
22. Aim to be liked
23. Wait for the conflict to recede on its own
24. Appeal to the people in charge

I		II		III		IV		V		VI	
1	___	2	___	3	___	4	___	5	___	6	___
7	___	8	___	9	___	10	___	11	___	12	___
13	___	14	___	15	___	16	___	17	___	18	___
19	___	20	___	21	___	22	___	23	___	24	___
TOTAL		TOTAL		TOTAL		TOTAL		TOTAL		TOTAL	

Conflict Resolution Styles

Direct/Controlling (Getting Our Way)

"My way or the highway." We do not, cannot, or will not bargain or give in. At times we are standing up for rights or beliefs that are important to us. We can also be pursuing what we want at the expense of others, or be unable to see a way to negotiate to get what we want.

Collaborating (Working It Out)

"Let's sit down and work this out." We work with others to find a way to get all of our needs met. We see the other people as partners, and spend time to find solutions to our conflict.

Compromising (Making a Deal)

"Let's both give a little" or "Something is better than nothing." Each party gives up something for a solution that may only meet some of our needs.

Accommodating (Giving In)

"Whatever you want is fine" or "It doesn't matter anyway." We yield to another, and meet another's needs but not our own. We may do this to keep a good relationship or to get our way another time.

Avoiding/Denying (Running Away)

"Let's skip it" or "Problem? I don't see a problem." We don't deal with the conflict, or we act as if the conflict isn't happening. We may leave others to deal with it.

Appealing to a Greater Authority or Third Party (Getting Help)

"Help me out here." We turn to others who may have more authority, influence, or skills in dealing with the conflict.

Conflict Styles in Literature

Directions: Think about the different ways to handle conflict. Write down how each character handled conflict and how helpful it was.

Character Name	Conflict Style	Examples of what the character did or said	Was the style helpful?

Chapter 4

Caring and Effective Communication

The ability to communicate is an essential skill for building relationships, creating classroom community, solving problems, and resolving conflict. Communication works best if the speaker is clear about what she is saying and if the listener listens attentively.

Good listening is one of the most important social skills students need to learn and develop. Too often, people are forming their responses before a speaker stops talking, especially in conflict situations, and not fully listening to the other person. Teaching students to understand the behaviors associated with active listening and to identify communication "blockers" that often get in the way are two of goals of this chapter.

In the midst of conflict situations, it is easy to think that our often emotionally charged responses are a way of telling the truth or being honest, but often they are simply attacks on the other person. For example, you-messages are statements that blame and attack another person ("You are always late"). Since the recipient often feels judged and condemned, a likely response is retaliation and counterattack, or withdrawal from the relationship — all damaging results. On the other hand, an I-message communicates the speaker's own wants, needs, or concerns ("I feel upset when I have to wait for you"). The receiver of the I-message learns how his behavior has affected the speaker. The receiver might still feel defensive, but communication is less likely to shut down completely. At its best, an I-message is assertive as opposed to aggressive; it's a relatively nonthreatening way to let others know how we feel and what we need.

The capacity to understand another person's point of view is essential to getting along with others and the most significant factor in developing a prosocial learning community. Understanding someone else's point of view enables people to develop empathy for those who are different. Activities that develop this skill enable students to increase their understanding of people and conflicts in two ways:

1. by raising students' awareness and understanding of the situations of others; and

2. by allowing students to gain a deeper emotional connection to others as they explore another person's feelings and perspective.

The tools introduced in this chapter that will help teach caring and effective communication are:

- Active Listening
- The PEAR Technique
- I-Messages
- Point of View

Tool: Active Listening

Explain that good listening requires us to pay attention to what someone is saying, and not to think about other things. Active Listening is a particular kind of listening that can help us to learn more about the needs of another person, understand a particular situation more fully, and help us to stay calm and focused when our emotions might be becoming engaged.

As an introduction, begin by modeling poor listening behaviors. Beforehand, plan a role-play with a student in which he tells you about a favorite movie or place to visit. Explain privately to the volunteer that you will be demonstrating poor listening, and that he should expect you to be inattentive, but should continue to speak. Role-play the scenario in front of the class. While the student is speaking, indicate with your body language that you are bored, tap your fingers, yawn, look out the window, look at your watch, interrupt with your own ideas, or use other distracting behaviors.

Ask the class what behaviors they noticed. Ask the student who was speaking what it was like to feel someone was not listening to him. Explain that the behaviors you exhibited are often called *communication blockers*. Then brainstorm a list of ideas that might help you to listen attentively next time, and record these on the board or on chart paper.

Ask the student to speak again, and model active, attentive listening behaviors. Be sure to:

- focus on the speaker (that can be shown by looking at the speaker, not looking elsewhere, and keeping one's body still)

- look interested in what is being said (smiling, nodding)

- ask questions to reaffirm what you hear or to find out more information

In a class discussion of the characteristics of active listening, complete a three-column chart and display it in the classroom as a reminder.

ACTIVE LISTENING

Looks Like	Sounds Like	Feels Like

Discuss communication blockers in more depth with older students. Role-play a second listening demonstration in which you prearrange a conversation with a student about a troubling issue. (This can be fictional, in order to not embarrass anyone.) Demonstrate the following communication blockers:

- Making jokes
  "Oh come on. You just need a few laughs. Did you hear about the..."

- Interrupting
  "Yeah, but listen to what Mary did to me."

- Changing the subject
  "Do you want to go shopping?"

- Criticizing the person's ideas
  "Oh great — that's just the craziest idea I ever heard."

- Blaming the person for her actions
  "I can't believe you did that. No wonder you're in trouble."

- Trying to solve the problem *for* the other person instead of *with* the other person
  "If I were you I'd..."
  "Don't take that from him."

Discuss with students the kinds of communication blockers they noticed in the role-play. Point out any they miss. Ask students to share, in pairs, their own experience with communication blockers and how it made them feel when people they were talking to used them. Then, have one student in each pair describe the same problem while the other practices Active Listening. Students can refer to the three-column chart during the practice.

How to Use the Active Listening Tool

- As a regular practice, place students in random pairings to discuss academic content and use Active Listening skills. For example, ask one student to talk to the other about an aspect of literature that the class is studying, and the partner to use the Active Listening skills that the class has developed.

- Examine the listening skills of characters in the literature the class is reading. Ask students to identify the communication blockers they find, and then rewrite selections to reflect ways the characters might have communicated if they had been active listeners.

- If characters in a selection are not using Active Listening, ask pairs of students to role-play what Active Listening would look like in this situation.

Tool: The PEAR Technique

The PEAR technique allows students to use Active Listening as a tool for dealing with intense feelings that may escalate a situation. The goal is to help students realize that there are Active Listening tools beyond merely attending to a speaker, and that these guidelines can help de-escalate conflict. The acronym PEAR stands for:

P   **Paraphrase** the facts (Say what you heard in your own words.):
- "So you want to buy a video game and your parents won't let you?"
- "You thought you were going to meet at your house before going to the rally."

E   **Encourage** the other person to talk:
- "I'm willing to listen to your side."
- "Do you want to talk this out?"

A   Pay **Attention**
- Look at the speaker.
- Encourage her by nodding or giving other positive signs.

R   **Reflect** feelings
- "You sound upset about not going to the party."
- "How do you feel when she says those kinds of things?"

One way to explore this concept is to use blank comic strips. In each frame, have two stick figures, each with a voice box. Write a situation in one voice box. For example, "I want to go to buy a video game and my parents are so mean and won't let me!" The second stick figure has an empty voice box. Have students write a response that practices the PEAR tool. For example, the second stick figure might paraphrase saying, "So, you want to buy a video game, but your parents won't let you?"

Discuss the situation with the students. Then have them role-play the situation, using all steps in the PEAR technique. Younger students can practice using PEAR in pairs. At the conclusion of the practice, ask speakers to tell the listeners what behavior was most effective at showing good listening.

How to Use the PEAR Tool

- When students have conflicts, suggest using PEAR to de-escalate the situation.

- Acknowledge students whom you notice using it on their own, and encourage them to continue. Any new tool is awkward at the beginning; fluency comes with practice.

- Many stories involve examples of poor communication or scenarios in which misunderstanding occurs because of a lack of communication. Ask students to look for communication blockers, and then rewrite scenes using the PEAR Tool. They can also role-play the scenario using the same technique.

- Continue to use the vocabulary associated with PEAR when discussing a selection. For example, "Did you notice Audra using *Encouraging* when she was listening to Raul?"

Tool: I-Messages

I-messages are one way students can take responsibility for their feelings and communicate their needs. This communication tool allows students to state their feelings to another person, describe what actions have led to those feelings, and explain why without attacking the other person. Instead of saying, "You are so sloppy. This place is always a mess. You need to stop it because I can't find any of my things anymore," an I-message might say, "<u>I feel</u> upset <u>when</u> the room has so many items lying around <u>because</u> I can't find my things."

The format is:

I feel _____
(state a feeling)

when _____
(describe the situation without judgment)

because _____
(state the effect this is having on you)

Since I-messages may seem artificial at first, it is important that students have many opportunities to practice them. Introducing the tool using a role-play can help students hear the difference between you-messages and I-messages. You might choose a scene like the previous example, in which one person attacks the other about his sloppiness, and the conflict escalates into shouting and meanness. Perform a second role-play, and have the first character speak strongly and assertively, using an I-message. For example, "I feel frustrated when there are so many things spread out over the room because I can't find anything." The other character should respond in a nondefensive manner, saying, "I'm sorry you feel that way. It doesn't seem that messy to me, but maybe we could work on figuring out how we can both feel OK in here." Discuss ways the characters can problem solve, instead of fight. Explain that the intention of using I-messages is not to get someone to do what you want them to do, but to "open the door" to problem solving. The other person always has the choice to participate or not, but at least the choice has been offered.

List a series of statements on an overhead projector, including both you- and I-messages. Have students work in pairs to identify which statements are you-messages and which are I-messages. Ask them to rewrite the you-messages as I-messages. If students comment that the I-messages seem phony or artificial, explain that learning a new skill often feels awkward, and that they may modify the statements once they understand the intent of an I-message.

Next, give each group of students a scenario that describes two parties beginning a conflict. Ask each group to write and perform two outcomes for the scenario, one with a you-message and then an I-message.

How to Use the I-Message Tool

- Encourage students to use I-messages in everyday situations, especially when they would like to work on problem solving with a friend or family member.

- Many stories have examples of blaming statements. Ask students to identify these statements and then to rewrite scenes having the characters use I-messages.

- Point out instances of literary characters speaking in an assertive way, perhaps even modifying the I-message format. Encourage students to modify the format themselves, while still being sure that their statements are not blaming.

Tool: Point of View

Recognizing and acknowledging other points of view is an essential skill for resolving conflict. Although students may have difficulty understanding or even identifying another person's perspective, practice through literature and other activities can help them to become more skillful. Once students understand that we all see the world differently, it is possible to increase empathy and de-escalate the conflict. Discuss how boring the world would be if we all agreed on everything. Remind students that progress is often a result of disagreement with the status quo.

Many activities can explain Point of View to students. One method uses pictures that can be interpreted differently. There are several pictures available on popular web sites that show different images, depending on how you view the picture, such as Old Woman/Young Woman, Duck/Rabbit, and Urns/Faces. The Old Woman/Young Woman example is included at the end of this chapter. Choose a picture and show it on an overhead or pass out copies. Have students work in pairs to tell each other what they see. Once everyone can see both of the images, ask if there was one "correct" image. Explain that just as different people saw different images, people often see conflicts from two entirely different points of view. This is what can make problem solving difficult.

Older students can explore the concept of Point of View Glasses. Explain that each of us sees the world through an invisible pair of sunglasses that can be called the Point of View Glasses. Everything we see and experience is filtered through these glasses. Draw a large pair of glasses on the board, and brainstorm with students what "lenses" we use to see the world. Be sure to include many different ideas, such as our experiences, where we live, values we think are important, feelings we have. The lenses change as we get older and have more experiences. Some of the lenses are visible to others, such as our age and our gender, but others are not necessarily obvious, such as our values and our experiences. Explain that because we each see the world through a unique set of Point of View Glasses, sometimes two or more people can see the same thing very differently. This can result in a conflict in which we assume that one side is seeing a "correct" version of things, and the other is "wrong." If we're not willing to try to understand another point of view, it can make problem solving very difficult.

How to Use the Point of View Tool

- When reading literature, encourage students to "stand in the shoes" of the characters and discuss what happened from their point of view.

- Invite students to talk and write about how they would feel if they were in a particular character's situation. If you've used the Point of View Glasses metaphor, have them draw the glasses and label the lenses through which the character sees the world.

- Encourage students to see the other point of view when they have a disagreement. Cut out two pairs of paper footprints. When two students have a conflict, ask them to stand on the "Point of View Footprints" and explain the problem from their point of view. Once each student has stated the problem, have them stand on the other person's footprints and restate the problem from the other point of view.

- When two characters are in a conflict, ask students to create Point of View Glasses for each one. Try to identify the "lenses" that might be involved in the conflict, such as differing cultural experiences. Then, ask students to write about how each character might communicate his or her point of view to the other character in a nonaggressive statement, perhaps with an I-message.

CLASSROOM
CONNECTION

In Ms. Jennifer's kindergarten classroom, Sally and Mary are having a disagreement over the dress-up clothes. They both end up in tears and cannot resolve the situation. Rather than placing the students in "time-out," Ms. Jennifer asks them what they might do to solve their problem. Mary suggests taking out the "magic slippers." Ms. Jennifer replies, "That's a good idea. Let's see what happens with the magic slippers. Maybe they can help us understand how each of you feels. We will take turns wearing the magic slippers." Ms. Jennifer has decorated these slippers with beads and stars. Mary puts on the slippers and describes the problem from her point of view. She wants to be able to wear the pink dress because she hasn't had a turn yet. She is encouraged not to use blaming statements. Sally then wears the slippers and tells about the conflict from her point of view. "I just got to put the dress on and I want to wear it longer." The slippers go back on the first child and Ms. Jennifer asks, "Do you understand what Sally is saying? Can you tell what Sally is feeling?" Ms. Jennifer is trying to have Sally understand Mary's perspective. The second child repeats the wearing of the slippers as she states the point of view of the other girl. The activity ends with an agreement. The first child will have the dress for two more minutes, and then the second child will have the dress for five minutes.

LINKS TO
LITERATURE

The True Story of the Three Little Pigs

Jon Scieszka

New York: Puffin Books, 1996 • Grade Level: K-4

Jon Scieszka writes the story of the three little pigs from the wolf's perspective. A. Wolf claims that it's not his fault that wolves are carnivores. He tries to gain sympathy by stating that he did not threaten any of the pigs; he had to sneeze each time he was waiting at the door for someone to answer. When the houses of the first two pigs fell down due to his terrible sneezes, he had two wonderful dinners, since it would be silly just to leave a ham dinner lying there. The pig in the third house was supposedly so rude to A. Wolf that it put him into a rage, which is what the police saw when they arrived at the scene.

 Active Listening Tool: In pairs, ask students to take turns talking about a time when they couldn't see the point of view of another person, just as it is hard for people to see A. Wolf's perspective in the traditional fairy tale. The listener should try to practice Active Listening skills.

 PEAR Tool: Have students work in pairs, with one being A.Wolf and the other the policeman who arrives at the end of the story. Each should tell his point of view while the other uses PEAR.

 I-message Tool: Have students write I-messages that the pigs might say to the wolf when they are about to be eaten.

Point of View Tool: Have students rewrite other traditional fairy tales from the point of view of other characters.

The Pain and the Great One

Judy Blume

New York: Dragonfly Books, 1985   •   Grade Level: K-4

This is a book about sibling rivalry, in which a brother (the Pain) and a sister (The Great One) view life in the same household from two very different points of view. In the first portion of the book, the sister is telling her story about her younger brother. She feels that he is treated much better than she, and describes a multitude of examples, such as how dad carries him in the kitchen in the morning, and helps him so he's not late for the school bus. Mom takes glory in his schoolwork, and he gets dessert when he doesn't eat all of his dinner. The second part of the story, The Great One, is told from the little brother's perspective. He describes things differently. He thinks his sister thinks she's so great because she can play the piano, work the can opener, baby-sit for their aunt, and remember phone numbers.

 Active Listening Tool: Divide students in pairs. Choose an incident from the story to talk about. Have one student take the role of the brother and the other the sister. First have them talk to each other without listening, using the communication blockers the class discussed. Next, have one speak while the other uses Active Listening, and then reverse roles. At the conclusion, ask pairs to give feedback about what their partners did well when they were listening.

 PEAR Tool: Using the steps of PEAR, have students rewrite a part of the story in which The Pain and The Great One use communication blockers. The rewrite would involve the characters choosing to listen in order to de-escalate a situation. An alternative to this activity is to have students role-play the scenario using the PEAR Tool.

 I-Message Tool: Choose a conflict from the story, and ask students to rewrite it, with the characters using I-messages to communicate their feelings and experiences.

Point of View Tool: In groups, ask students to create two Point of View Glasses, one for The Pain and one for The Great One. (See handout at end of chapter) Each pair of glasses should illustrate the lenses through which the character sees the world.

Taking Care of Terrific

Lois Lowry

New York: Yearling, 1984 • Grade Level: 3-7

Enid, a fourteen-year-old girl, takes a summer job babysitting Joshua Cameron IV. Joshua has been overprotected by his mother as much as Enid has been ignored by hers. However, this summer, Enid has decided that it is time for a change. Enid and Joshua spend each day at the Boston Public Garden, where they make new friends, including an old bag lady, a hawk, and a saxophonist.

 **Active Listening, PEAR, and I-Message Tools:** Have students refer to pp. 40-45 in the book. Divide the class into groups of four or five. First, have each group identify all of the communication blockers they can find in the segment. Then, ask them to rewrite the dinner table scene using applicable components of the PEAR Tool and I-messages. Have them rehearse their scenes and perform them for the class.

 Point of View Tool: Each of the characters that Enid and Joshua meet can provide an activity for exploring Point of View because each has unique life experiences. Stop at various points during the story and have students create Point of View Glasses for the characters. (Use handout at end of chapter).

From Slave Ship to Freedom Road

Julius Lester

New York: Puffin Books, 1999   •   Grade Level: 5+

The historically correct art work that accompanies the story inspired Lester to write about slavery. Lester describes the slave experience, beginning with transport aboard three-masted ships to the auction block, and on to the plantation fields. The text is written in such a way that readers "step into" the artwork and imagine themselves as slaves.

 Active Listening Tool: Divide students in pairs. Ask them to pretend they are a part of one of Rod Brown's paintings, and to describe what they see and hear to their partner. Their partner should practice Active Listening and ask questions to find out more.

 PEAR Tool: Place students in pairs and have one take on the role of a slave owner and the other the role of a friend of his. Ask the slave owner to take the role of someone who is not sure that his occupation is a moral one, but who feels that his dependence on slaves for business reasons is necessary. His friend should try to stay nonjudgmental and use the PEAR Tool.

 I-Message Tool: Ask students to choose a situation described in the text and create an I-message for the slaves involved.

Point of View Tool: Lester's purpose is to lead the reader from painting to painting and ask questions that evoke empathy. Sometimes the questions are for the white people, and sometimes they are for the slaves. Lester writes about his own deep emotions and imagines what it would have been like to be a slave, and invites the reader to do the same. Invite students to "step into" the point of view of the slaves, as well as the slave owners. Ask students to explore the following: How could a slave owner justify owning slaves? What was the prevailing thought about this situation? How would a slave feel about being forced to leave his country?

Chrysanthemum

Kevin Henkes

New York: HarperTrophy, 1996
Grade Level: K-3

Chrysanthemum is proud of her musical sounding name until she goes to kindergarten and is tormented by others. The popular music teacher, who has an unusual name herself — Delphinium — tells her students she plans to name her expected baby the prettiest name she has heard, Chrysanthemum.

Through Grandpa's Eyes

Patricia MacLachlan

HarperTrophy, 1983
Grade Level: K-3

During John's visits to Grandpa's house, he learns about the special ways his blind grandfather sees and moves in the world.

Albert's Impossible Toothache

Barbara Williams

Cambridge, MA: Candlewick Press, 2003, 1974
Grade Level: K-3

No one will believe that Albert has a toothache; turtles don't have teeth. Then his grandmother asks Albert where he has the toothache and finds out a gopher had bitten Albert's left toe.

How Jackrabbit Got His Very Long Ears

Heather Irbinskas

Flagstaff, AZ: Northland, 2004
Grade Level: K-3

After creating the desert creatures, the Great Spirit assigns Jackrabbit to acquaint the animals with their new homes. Because he doesn't listen carefully, Jackrabbit gives incorrect information to Tortoise, Bobcat, and Roadrunner. This harms their self-esteem. So the Great Spirit affirms the creatures and gives Jackrabbit ears that will help him in the future.

A Quiet Place

Douglas Wood

New York: Aladdin, 2005
Grade Level: K-3

The book suggests many places where a child can find quiet, including books and his own solitude.

Bat in the Dining Room

Crescent Dragonwagon

New York: Marshall Cavendish, 2003, 1997
Grade Level: K-3

Observant Melissa thinks about how a bat feels when it lands in the dining room of a hotel. While everyone else panics, she keeps her cool and leads the bat back into the night.

Meanest Thing to Say

Bill Cosby

New York: Scholastic, 2004, 1997
Grade Level: K-3

Michael Reilly cannot get Little Bill to join him in saying mean things. Bill and his friends say, "So?" and later invite Michael to play with them.

The Three Little Wolves and the Big, Bad Pig

Eugene Trivizas

New York: Scholastic, 1994
Grade Level: K-5

The three little wolves, who were warned about the big bad pig, construct their first house out of sturdy brick. It resists the pig's huffing and puffing, but not his sledgehammer. The wolves build stronger and stronger houses, but the pig's destructive methods keep up. Then the wolves weave a house of flowers. The fragrance tames the pig so much that he and the wolves live together happily ever after.

Pirate's Eye

Robert Priest

Boston: Houghton Mifflin, 2005
Grade Level: 2-4

Captain Black loses his glass eye, and Sandpiper, an artistic pauper, finds it. When Sandpiper sees images in the eye, he writes a book about Black's life, and then returns the eye to the captain. Black reforms his life when he sees in the eye the kindness of Sandpiper's life.

Speak to Me (And I Will Listen between the Lines)

Karen English

New York: Farrar Straus Giroux, 2004
Grade Level: 3-5

The book showcases poems by six young students that reveal what is going on in their lives.

Old Woman/ Young Woman

Point of View Glasses

Directions: Each of us looks at the world from our own point of view, like looking through glasses, called Point of View (POV) glasses. Use the glasses below to illustrate a person's or character's point of view. Cut out and ask students to try on new points of view using the glasses.

Chapter 5

Cultural Competence and Alliance Building

Students today can look forward to a culturally-rich future. Their connection to the world is one that previous generations could not even conceive of. Worldwide instant communication and information have created opportunities for us all to know and learn more about other cultures than was ever thought possible. Differences, however, can lead to challenges, and misunderstanding other cultures, making assumptions, and negative stereotyping, for example, can lead to conflicts that are difficult to address. The goal is to provide experiences for students that will allow them to truly appreciate differences while dealing with the challenges that can arise when people from different cultures live and work together.

Creating an environment in which cultures are valued and explored, and differences are celebrated, will stimulate discussions that lead to understanding others. When students are allowed to share their heritage with others, the "unknown" becomes more familiar and thus more comfortable.

Students also need to see themselves as part of the classroom environment. Can students find their culture in pictures, illustrations, and texts? Are their opinions accepted, even when they are in the minority? Is diversity welcomed, with all of its challenges, or is it a superficial exploration, limited to tastes of exotic foods and pigeonholing discussions of culture into "months" of celebration? Cultures need to be present, welcomed, and explored every day.

The skills introduced in previous chapters will help students to have positive experiences working with students who may be different from them. These positive experiences can undo dangerous stereotypes that children might have unconsciously picked up from others. However, students also need to become culturally competent and understand the vocabulary that encompasses issues around differences, such as *stereotypes* and *discrimination*. To be culturally competent, one must be able first to examine one's own prejudices, recognize the structures in society that reinforce these prejudices, and acknowledge the obligation to interrupt acts of discrimination that one may encounter.

The tools introduced in this chapter will help students become more skillful in speaking up. They will also provide experiences for students to examine their similarities and differences, and work to value, rather than judge them. This will further the goal of a classroom of learners who are finding out what it means to be culturally competent. The tools in this chapter include:

- Venn Diagram

- Opinion Continuum

- Brainstorming

Tool: Venn Diagram

A Venn Diagram provides a framework for examining similarities and differences. It is a helpful first step in naming and dealing with differences because it avoids judging these differences. To introduce it, start by brainstorming a list of categories or questions that students can ask each other in order to discover the ways in which they are alike and different. A list of questions might include: What do you like to do in your spare time? Do you have any pets? What's your favorite food? Categories might include food, hobbies, favorites, etc. Pair students randomly. An easy way to do this is by distributing playing cards or postcards that have been cut in half, and inviting students to match the halves to find their partners. This format prevents students from being left out, which can happen if students find partners without using concrete materials. Next, have each pair draw two circles that overlap on a piece of paper. You might prepare a handout if you think the students will have difficulty with this. In the overlap area, the pairs will list things they have in common, and in the outer part of each of the circle, the attributes that are unique to each individual. Have students answer the questions the class brainstormed and fill in the Venn Diagram with their partner. Students who do not yet write can draw pictures.

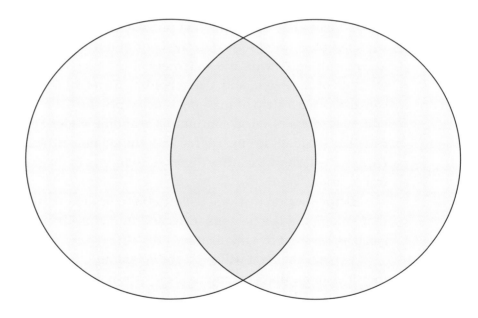

Form a circle with the students, and in a go-round, have each pair tell the class about their Venn diagram. Be sure to post the results. Ask students what was interesting about the activity. Did anything surprise them? Was this easy or difficult? Can differences with others sometimes be challenging? Do we need to be the same as others in order to get along with them or be friends with them? How can we show respect to people who are different from us?

- Continue to use this tool with pairs of students throughout the year in order for students to learn about as many of their classmates as possible.

- Have students choose two characters in a book and create a Venn Diagram that shows their differences and similarities. Then ask them to share it with a partner. Older students can include the characters' values and opinions in their diagrams.

- If a book has more than one setting, ask students to create a Venn Diagram to compare and contrast various settings.

Tool: Opinion Continuum

When students disagree with each other, or when they hold differing beliefs and values, it can be hard to maintain good relationships. Work with the class to explore the idea that people can hold different opinions from their classmates and friends and still have a positive relationship. This idea can help create a harmonious classroom in which differences are respected and welcomed.

Explain that in an Opinion Continuum a series of statements are read and students place themselves on the continuum depending on how much they agree or disagree with the statement. Tape a sign reading *Strongly Agree* on one side of the room, and a sign reading *Strongly Disagree* on the other. You can also place a strip of masking tape across the floor, with the signs at either end, to create a physical continuum. Standing under *Strongly Agree* will indicate that students strongly agree with the statement. Standing under *Strongly Disagree* will show that they disagree. Standing in the middle will show a neutral position.

Before beginning the activity, discuss the definition of an opinion. Explain that an opinion is a person's ideas and thoughts about something; it is a personal assessment or judgment.

Explain that you will say a statement and then students will decide how they feel about that statement. If they strongly agree with the statement, they will stand under the sign that says *Strongly Agree*. If they strongly disagree, they will stand under the sign that says *Strongly Disagree*. They may also stand somewhere in between to show varying degrees of agreement or disagreement. Once everyone is in place, the class will see a variety of opinions. Reiterate that there are no right or wrong answers and that each person should decide for himself how he feels about the statement before moving. Explain that sometimes people are tempted to go along with what their friends think, but if people do this during this activity, it will make it impossible to see the differences in the room. If, however, students do follow each other, it's best not to point this out. Once students who are not comfortable with the exercise see that you allow them to find their comfort level and are not judging them, they tend to be braver in stating their own opinions.

Read the first statement. *The best flavor of ice cream is vanilla.* Ask students to find their places on the continuum. This is a good warm-up, since it will be easy for students to "take a stand" on this subject. Then ask a few students who are standing in various places on the continuum why they chose to stand where they did.

Repeat this process with each of the following statements, or substitute statements based on your knowledge of students' interests. Ask students to stand in the place that reflects their opinion, and then have a few share why they chose to stand where they did. If students begin speaking up against someone else's opinion, remind them that this is a time to share opinions, not judge them, and that we can respect different opinions without agreeing with them.

Statements

1. The best pet is a dog.

2. Math is more fun than reading.

3. The best thing to do on vacation is to go camping.

The intention of this activity is to allow students to see that people have different opinions about these statements. Since there are no wrong or right answers, avoid commenting or sharing your own perspective on the statements. Have students return to their seats, or to a circle. Ask students:

- Was it hard to decide where to stand?

- Were there any times when it was harder for you to decide where to stand?

- Was there a time when you were standing in a different place from a friend of yours? When?

- When you want to tell someone that you don't share her opinion, what is a respectful way to say that? (Be careful not to attack the opinion; instead, say, "I disagree with....")

How to Use the Opinion Continuum Tool

- Use the opinion continuum to explore how students feel about a particular text. Use the statement, "I like reading about _____ (the topic of the book)." Ask students to stand on the continuum to express their opinion. Once they have disclosed their opinions about the book that the class is reading, ask about other topics. Ask them to agree or disagree (or anywhere on the continuum) that fiction is the best kind of book to read. One example that will enliven debate is: Comic books are not really works of literature.

- The opinion continuum can also be used for making predictions when reading a book. Stop at an appropriate point, offer a possible outcome, and ask students to place themselves on the opinion continuum. If they think the outcome will happen, they can stand near *Strongly Agree*. If they don't think it will happen, they should stand near *Strongly Disagree*. Ask them to share the reasons for their choice with the person next to them. Then ask for volunteers to share their reasons with the class.

- To examine the motivations of characters, ask students to stand on the opinion continuum to show if they agree or disagree with a character's actions. Again, it is important that students can explain why they have chosen their response, and perhaps to give examples from the story that support their decision.

Tool: Brainstorming

Brainstorming, done in an open, accepting way, can provide a technique that enables students to free themselves from seeing one right way of doing or thinking about things, and to broaden their repertoire of strategies and responses in dealing with other people. An important part of developing students' cultural competence is to acknowledge that there is not one "right" way to interact with others, or to deal with divisive issues. It can be tempting to lecture students on what they *should do* in a particular instance, or how people *shouldn't be prejudiced*. However, lectures rarely have much effect. They are often discounted by students as examples of our not understanding what their experience is like, and students may also just tune us out and only pretend to listen.

Brainstorming should allow a free flow of ideas, without judgment. Too often, teachers begin brainstorming with students and make comments about their contributions or allow them to judge each other's contributions. When students feel judged by their teacher or their classmates, they will be less likely to share their ideas.

The following activity uses brainstorming and role-playing to explore ways of interrupting bullying behavior:

1. Begin by asking if students have ever stood by and watched while someone was teased. How did this feel? What are reasons someone might not help out in a situation like this? Acknowledge that everyone can be fearful of becoming the target of teasing and that sometimes people

are embarrassed to say something in front of others. Then, divide students in pairs and ask them to exchange ideas with their partner about things people can do or say when they either witness or are involved in a teasing situation. Facilitate a brainstorming session with the entire class and list all ideas on the board without judgment. For example, if someone suggests hitting the person who is doing the teasing, simply add it to the brainstormed list. Once students see that you are not censoring their responses, they will be more comfortable sharing their ideas. Try to create a broad range of responses.

2. Ask students to think about which responses would not escalate the situation (see Chapter 3). Circle the responses that would make the situation better for everyone. After circling several possible solutions, have groups of students role-play each one for the class. Give each group the same specific scenario of a teasing situation and assign one response to each group to act out. Remind them that the response should not escalate the situation.

Helpful guidelines for role-plays are:

- Names of characters should not include the name of anyone in the class.

- No bad language.

- No touching; that should include any type of "pretend" fighting.

Other scenarios to brainstorm and role-play:

- One student calls another a name.

- A character is teased in front of others for some aspect of his appearance.

- A student makes mistakes while reading aloud in class, and becomes an object of ridicule by another classmate.

(It is helpful to create scenarios that you have seen or heard about at your school, but be careful not to target someone in the class.)

Have each group present their role-play to the class. Ask what was effective about the interventions that the participants acted out. If some of the choices actually escalate the conflict, ask if the class can suggest other alternatives.

Discuss the role-plays with the students. What was difficult about thinking up strategies? How did the brainstorming help? Acknowledge that learning new responses can sometimes be difficult, but can get easier with practice.

Often teachers and other adults can get in the habit of providing students with set responses to a situation, when in reality there may be many possible responses. Therefore, examining options when confronted with unfair situations is an important strategy for students to learn. If students brainstorm and practice many possible responses to real-life situations, they will feel the authenticity of this experience.

How to Use the Brainstorming Tool

- When reading a book, stop at specific points and brainstorm possible endings. Ask which ones are the most likely to happen. Students will need to give specific examples to justify their choices. For example, students might consider the events up to that point in the story, or the personalities and actions of the characters up to that point, or support their choice and predict possible outcomes.

- Before beginning a new book, invite students to think about the title and look at the artwork on the cover of the book. Brainstorm possible themes.

- When characters are in a conflict, stop and brainstorm possible paths the characters might take to resolve the conflict. Review the idea of win-win outcomes and ask students which solutions would qualify as win-win.

- When examining books that have a message about getting along with others, encourage students to brainstorm many possible options for various situations. For example, many books dealing with bullying and teasing promote just one or two responses to the behavior. Brainstorm additional responses that would be likely to result in a positive outcome.

LINKS TO LITERATURE

Chester's Way

Kevin Henkes

New York: HarperTrophy, 1997   •   Grade Level: K-3

Chester and Wilson are very much alike and very comfortable with their set routines. When Lilly moves into the neighborhood, they are put off at first by her outrageous behaviors. That is, until she rescues them from some bullies. Then they begin to realize what fun differences can be.

 Venn Diagram Tool: Ask students to create a Venn Diagram that compares Chester and Wilson. Then have them add a third circle that represents Lilly to see what the three have in common.

 Opinion Continuum Tool: Ask students to respond to statements that explore some of the activities the characters engage in, such as dancing and dressing in outrageous clothing.

 Brainstorming Tool: The Brainstorming Tool can open the discussion of the many things students like to do, and be a first step in sharing our cultures with each other. For example, brainstorm all of the things students like to do on vacation, or favorite foods students eat on particular holidays.

The Other Side of the Fence

Jacqueline Woodson

New York: Putnam Juvenile, 2001 • Grade Level: K-4

This book tells the story of two young girls, one white and one black, who live next door to each other and are separated by a fence. The girls notice their similarities, but are encouraged not to acknowledge each other by their friends and family. When one finally climbs the fence to sit beside the other, the fences of prejudice begin to crumble.

 Venn Diagram Tool: Have students explore the similarities and differences of the two characters in a Venn Diagram. Older students can also think about the nature of race relations and the demands of peer culture.

 Opinion Continuum Tool: Use the opinion continuum to have students think about prejudice and discrimination. Ask older students to respond to this statement: "People are not born with prejudices; they pick them up from their environment." If appropriate, follow with a class discussion. Younger students can discuss likes and dislikes, and the way we often don't like something before we even try it, just because we've heard something negative about it.

 Brainstorming Tool: Have students brainstorm possible options for the girl who wants to befriend the other, even when she is being discouraged from doing so. Or brainstorm ways we can approach others who may not be like us and become friends.

Joey Pigza Swallowed the Key

Jack Gantos

New York: HarperTrophy, 2000 • Grade Level: 3-8

Joey is a good kid who is unable to control his behavior and is medicated sporadically and unsuccessfully for attention deficit disorder. Reactions to his behavior range from frustration to bullying.

 Venn Diagram Tool: Have students create a Venn Diagram, with one circle representing Joey and the other themselves. Ask them to write down things that are true about Joey and things that are true about themselves. What traits do they share? Students can recognize similarities with Joey, and have empathy for the differences he struggles with.

 Opinion Continuum Tool: Use statements such as, "People with disabilities always have a wheelchair or cane," or "There are no famous people with disabilities," to elicit opinions for the opinion continuum. Be careful not to target particular students in the class, and instead deal in generalities that will spur lively conversation. You can also make statements about the text, such as, "Joey's teachers treated him very fairly," to elicit discussion about the story.

 Brainstorming Tool: Use the brainstorming tool to explore choices Joey has in responding to the way people treat him and to dealing with his frustration.

Black All Around!

Patricia Hubbel

New York: Lee & Low, 2004
Grade Level: K-3

A young girl celebrates as she discovers the color black in all areas of life.

The Skin You Live in

Michael Tyler

Chicago, IL: Chicago Children's Museum, 2005
Grade Level: K-3

A poem with whimsical illustrations celebrates our skin in its usefulness and variations.

Watch Out for These Weirdos!

Rufus Kline

New York: Puffin, 1992
Grade Level: 1-4

The narrator describes a group of characters in the neighborhood who happen to be his friends.

What Lies on the Other Side?

Udo Weigelt

Translated by J. Alison James

New York: North-South, 2002
Grade Level: K-4

Little Fox is afraid of the witches and dragons on Raccoon's side of the river, and Raccoon is afraid of the giants and robbers on Fox's side. When they show each other around and explain the origins of the rumors, the animals on both sides of the river become friends.

My Diary from Here to There

Amanda Irma Perez

San Francisco: Children's Book Press, 2002
Grade Level: 1-4

Young Amanda tells of her family's move from Juarez, Mexico, to Los Angeles. Her diary helps her cope with the loss of her friend Michi and the strangeness of a new land and language.

Skin Again

bell hooks

New York: Hyperion, 2005
Grade Level: K-4

Each person has a story that is more than skin deep. "The skin I'm in will always be just a covering. It cannot tell my story."

Baseball Saved Us

Ken Mochizuki

New York: Lee & Low Books, 1995
Grade Level: 1-4

In a World War II internment camp, a young Japanese-American boy and his father build a baseball diamond and form a league so that the internees will have something to look forward to -– even if only for nine innings.

Harvesting Hope: The Story of Cesar Chavez

Kathleen Krull

San Diego, CA: Harcourt Children's Books, 2003
Grade Level: 1-6

When Cesar Chavez was ten years old, drought forced his family to leave their ranch and move to California, where they became migrant workers who worked in terrible living conditions and were paid low wages. When Chavez became an adult, he worked for worker's rights and organized a nonviolent revolt, producing the first farm workers' union contract.

Teammates

Peter Golenbock

Orlando, FL: Voyager Books, 1992
Grade Level: 1-6

This picture book, with both color illustrations and black and white photos, is the story of how Jackie Robinson became the first black player on a major league baseball team, and how PeeWee Reese took a stand and declared Jackie his teammate.

My Name Is Bilal

Asma Mobin-Uddin

Honesdale, PA: Boyds Mills Press, 2005
Grade Level: 3-6

Bilal stands by as his sister Ayesha is harassed by Scott because of her head scarf. He decides to use the name Bill Al in class, but his Muslim teacher gives him a book about his namesake, an ancient Muslim prayer leader. Later Bilal invites Scott to join a basketball game and the two play together until an older student, who is Muslim, leaves to pray and Bilal joins him.

Appendix
Reading Strategies

The reading strategies outlined in this appendix are designed to provide further experiences that will integrate literacy development with social and emotional learning. Each strategy is defined, then followed by suggestions of how and when to use it.

STRATEGY

Sketch to Stretch
(Harste, Short, & Burke, 1988)

Sketch to Stretch is designed to have students represent what they have read in a visual format. Because there may be different interpretations of a text, this technique can help students understand different points of view when interpreting literature.

STEPS:

1. Provide students with paper, pencils, crayons, or markers.

2. Ask students to think about the text they have read or that has been read to them, and draw a sketch of what the selection meant to them. The drawing can be done in pictures or in symbols. Be sure to select a text that appropriately addresses a specific issue so students can develop skills related to it. For example, if the goal is to have students explore possible win-win solutions to a conflict, make sure the text includes a conflict. Emphasize to students that the focus is on the drawing's meaning and not on their artistic abilities.

3. Have students share their sketches with a small group of four or five of their peers. Each member of the group offers an interpretation of the text, then the student who created the drawing explains what it meant to her. Continue until each member of the group has had a turn.

4. Ask students to gather as a whole group. Guide them in a conversation about different interpretations of a text, and discuss the fact that some interpretations were alike and some were different. Stress that no one is "right" or "wrong," but that each person can interpret the same information differently, and that is their point of view.

5. Students from different groups could share their drawings with the group or on the overhead projector. Again, class members must interpret the illustration before the artist shares her interpretation. Accept all logical interpretations of text.

STRATEGY
#2

Visualization
(Gambrell & Bales, 1986)

Visualization, or induced imagery, is a process that increases students' reading comprehension and helps them develop empathy for characters in a story. It allows students to identify with characters by seeing them in their mind's eye as they read and/or replay story events.

STEPS:

1. Explain to students that sometimes when they are reading they can make pictures in their minds about what they are reading.

2. Think aloud for the students: "When we read what is happening, and picture what is read, it is like watching a movie. We see what is happening to characters in the story and begin to understand how they feel."

3. Have the students close their eyes. Tell them a portion of the story. Ask them to pretend that they are looking at a large movie screen. On that movie screen they can see the passage they have just heard. Model the visualization for the students by saying, "When I look at the movie screen in my head, I see... ."

4. Have students share their visualization with a partner or in small groups.

5. Students can also visualize content lessons. For example, after reading about factory workers during the British Industrial Revolution, ask students to visualize the working conditions.

STRATEGY
#3

Semantic Feature Analysis Grid
(Heimlich & Pittman, 1986)

A Semantic Feature Analysis Grid is a chart that compares similarities and differences between members of a specific category, such as characters in a story. (Pittelman, Heimlich, Berglund, & French, 1991). A main benefit of a Semantic Feature Analysis Grid is the discussion that accompanies it. For example, the grid can serve as a catalyst for discussion about the traits of characters in a story, can foster understanding of different points of view, and can help students analyze those character traits that help to manage conflict as well to analyze the characteristics that foster it.

STEPS:

1. Select the main characters from a reading selection. Write the names of the characters in the left hand side of the grid.

2. Across the top of the grid write down character traits that some, but not all, of the characters possess. Allow students to add characters and character traits as they read the story. For example:

	Character Traits		
	Honesty	Caring	Trustworthiness
Phoebe			
Salamanca			
Gram			
Mrs. Winterbottom			

3. At the end of the book, or after reading a selection, stop and review the characters and character traits. Students will need to decide as a group if each character possesses the traits listed. If students agree that a character possesses the trait listed, put a (+) in the column. If students do not think the character possesses the trait, put a (-) in the column. If there is no agreement, place a (+) and a (-) in the column.

STRATEGY
#4

Character Clusters
(Macon, Bewell, & Voght, 1991)

A character cluster is a semantic map that identifies character traits and also identifies the rationale for the classification. It helps students compare characters and promotes discussion. By creating a character cluster, students will also begin to see how a person's actions shape the way others view them.

STEPS:

1. Draw a circle/oval in the middle of the board or on an overhead transparency.

2. Write the name of the character in the middle of the oval.

3. Ask students to think of or write words that describe the character and share them out loud.

4. Write these descriptors outside the main oval and connect them to the character's name.

5. Finally, ask students to justify their responses by identifying behaviors that are examples of the character traits described.

6. Students can draw character clusters for more than one character in the story. Each character cluster can be connected to an oval containing the title of the story.

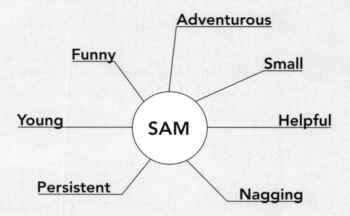

The Literature Chart
(Roser & Hoffman, 1995)

The Literature Chart is an organizer that helps students analyze the elements in a story. It can help them understand conflict by comparing story elements in various texts. Story elements in this case will consist of the title, characters, problem, solution, and ending.

STEPS:

1. Select at least three books that have clearly identified conflicts that are resolved.

2. Have students read one story and identify all of the elements (title, characters, problem, solution, and ending) and put them in chart form.

3. Emphasize that there was a conflict in the story and focus on the way the conflict was solved.

4. Read the next story. After a discussion, complete the chart for the second story. Ask questions that help students understand that in both stories conflict was resolved. This will help students realize that conflict is a normal part of life and that conflicts can be solved.

5. Add the third and final book to the chart. Continue conversations, helping students understand that conflicts are not all bad.

6. Have students compare and contrast the conflicts in each book and the ways in which they were solved.

7. Hang up the chart where students can refer to it.

STRATEGY

Think-Alouds
(Pressley, et. al., 1989 & 1992)

A think-aloud is an exercise in which the teacher makes his thinking explicit by verbalizing his thoughts while reading — he "thinks out loud" for the students. It is one of the core components of good teacher modeling, enabling teachers to model the manner in which students can relate a story to something that has happened in their life, to the world, or to another text. This develops empathy, as the students begin to see that they have something in common with characters, settings, or problems.

STEPS:

1. Select a book that is age-appropriate and that has a conflict students can relate to.

2. Pick one or more specific stopping points in advance. Read up to the first stopping point. Put the book on your lap and start describing a time when something happened to you that relates to the story. For example, if you were reading the story *Amazing Grace* you might say, "I remember a time when I wanted to be in a school play but I didn't try out for it because I was afraid everyone would laugh at me. I think Grace might feel a little discouraged because the students in the class are saying she can't play Peter Pan."

3. Continue to read up to the next stopping point. Describe a situation in your life that relates to the story.

4. Ask the students if any parts of the story remind them of something that happened in their own life.

5. Continue modeling the think-aloud strategy until the students begin to make connections on their own.

6. Once students seem to understand the concept of text-to-self connections, you can model text-to-text and text-to-world connections. For example, a text-to-text connection would be, "I was just thinking about the story, *Oliver Button is a Sissy*. I was thinking that Oliver and Grace were alike because they both had the courage to keep doing what they liked, even though other students thought they were different. Can you think of any other ways that Oliver and Grace were alike? How were they different? What connections can you share between the two stories?" A text-to-world think-aloud may be, "I was watching the news last night and I saw that women in some countries have to cover their faces. They are not allowed to go outside unless they are covered. I don't think that these women would get the chance to try to be Peter Pan. I think it might be hard for me to live there."

STRATEGY

#7

Word Walls
(Cunningham, 2000)

Word Walls consist of key vocabulary words that students have learned in class and are written on a chart that is displayed on a wall. Students can refer to the Word Wall in their conversations and in their writing. Word Walls can be written on tagboard, butcher paper, white board, etc. They can be organized around particular themes. For the purposes of social and emotional learning, it is helpful to have vocabulary related to feelings as a focus for a Word Wall.

STEPS:

1. Decide where you want to display the Word Wall. It should be in a highly visible area. Write the words large enough so that students don't have to leave their seats to read them.

2. Decide on a theme and organizational scheme; for example, Feelings Words.

3. Read a book or a series of books that focus on the selected theme. For example, if the theme is Feelings Words, select texts that illustrate many emotions. Discuss new words that either you identify while reading, or that students identify as they read. Categorize them and write them on the Wall.

4. Encourage children to refer to the Word Wall for everyday situations. For example, if the theme is Feelings, they can practice using the words to express themselves better.

Anticipation Guide
(Readance, Bean, & Baldwin, 1982, and Head & Readance, 1986)

Anticipation Guides direct attention to the main ideas of a reading selection, and provide students the opportunity to use their communication skills and listen to different points of view. Students will read statements before and after a reading selection and agree or disagree with the statement. Prior to reading, students react to statements based on their background knowledge and/or feelings, and make an intelligent guess or prediction about the statement's validity. During the postreading phase, students must respond based on the text content and support their answers by referring to the passage.

STEPS:

1. Determine the main ideas and supporting details of the text that students will read or that you will read to the students.

2. Select three to five main idea statements and write a sentence for each.

3. Identify student experiences that you feel will elicit the most responses from the group.

    For example, if you were teaching a history lesson on the British Industrial Revolution, a statement such as "Children were made to work 12-hour days, 7 days a week in factories," would stimulate conversation as students discussed whether they think this is a true statement.

4. Arrange the statements on a sheet of paper, overhead transparency, or on the board.

5. Have students respond to each statement individually. For younger students, a smiling or frowning face can be used. Older students can record their justification for each response, so they will have a reference point for discussion.

6. Your role as a teacher is that of a facilitator. First, ask who agrees with the statement, and why, or who thinks the statement is true, and why. Ask students to justify their responses. Next ask who disagrees

with the statement, or thinks that it is false, and have students justify their answers. This step provides students with the opportunity to use I-messages and Active Listening skills as they listen to one another's point of view.

7. Following the discussion of all the statements, ask the students to read the selection (or read it out loud to them) to determine which statements were actually true and which were false. Their answers must be justified by their readings. This provides students with a reason for reading the selection and helps them focus on the main ideas of the passage.

STRATEGY #9

Open-Mind Portraits
(Tompkins, 2003)

An Open-Mind Portrait gives students the opportunity to reflect on story events from a character's point of view. It helps them identify with the character's feelings, attitudes, and point of view.

STEPS:

1. Draw a portrait of a character from the book, including the head and neck.

2. On the back of the portrait, draw pictures that describe what the character might be thinking/feeling.

3. This drawing could be done three times, one each for how the character thinks/feels at the beginning, middle, and end of the book.

STRATEGY #10

Say Something
(Harste, Short, & Burke, 1988)

Say Something enables students to work collaboratively to comprehend text better. Students work in pairs to read a text, stopping at predetermined stopping points to talk to one another about what they have read.

STEPS:

1. Select a text that is somewhat challenging. This will motivate students to work together to comprehend the selection. Be sure that the book is engaging enough that the students will be motivated to read.

2. Select stopping points in advance. Stop prior to exciting events to hold students' interest and to help them build skills for making predictions.

3. Divide students into pairs. You may determine the pairs any way you wish, depending on the textual demands of the reading. For example, you may want to pair a stronger reader with a struggling reader.

4. Each pair can decide how they want to read the text. They may want to silent read, oral read, mumble read, echo read, etc.

5. Direct the students to read until the first stopping point. Tell them that when they reach that point they should talk about what they have read. Go over communication skills at this time.

6. Repeat the process until the selection is complete.

7. Following the reading, ask the students what they talked about at the stopping points. Categorize their responses on the board. For example, if a pair of students reported that they discussed what was going to happen next, you would write Predictions on the board.

    Review the list of reading strategies that the students used on their own as a result of the Say Something strategy.

STRATEGY
#11

Directed Listening/Thinking Activity
(Stauffer, 1975)

The Directed Listening/Thinking Activity is a strategy used to engage students in making predictions prior to and during the reading of a text. Making predictions is an important skill that keeps readers involved in a story, activates their background knowledge, and allows them to make inferences about the text. This strategy also engages students in problem solving.

STEPS:

1. Select a story with an exciting plot so that students will want to make predictions about major story events at predetermined stopping points.

2. Select two to four stopping points. Be sure to select the stopping points prior to reading about an exciting event. This will encourage students to make predictions.

3. Introduce the text to the students. If you are using a picture book, read the title of the story and have students examine the illustrations on the front cover. If you are using a chapter book, you may read an introductory passage or the first chapter. Provide enough information to enable students to make a logical prediction about the text.

4. Use guided questions as necessary. For example, "What do you see on the front cover?" "Why do you think the character is doing what he is doing?" Reread the title and ask the students what they think the text is about.

5. Praise all responses. It is helpful to say, "That might happen," since you don't want to favor one prediction over another. Encourage students to draw inferences and to appreciate one another's ideas, not to determine whose prediction is accurate or "better."

6. Record all predictions on the board or chart paper. Ask students how they came up with their predictions.

7. Read the story up to the first stopping point, or if the students are able, have them read the text. Have students summarize what has happened in the story up the stopping point. Have them review their original predictions and alter them accordingly. Then ask the students if they would like to make new predictions. At no time should a prediction be linked to a specific child; for example, "Johnny's prediction... ."

8. Continue until you come to the end of the story. Discuss the entire selection, focusing on story elements such as setting, characters, conflict, conflict solution (if there is one), and the ending.
   The Directed Listening/Thinking Activity can also be used to focus on problem solving. Choose stopping points prior to a solution to a conflict. Ask students to use the problem solving method:

   • Ask what the problem is.
   • Brainstorm solutions.
   • Choose a solution they think might work.

9. Compare and contrast the character's solution with the solutions students suggested. Ask them if their solutions may have worked and have them explain their responses.

STRATEGY
#12

Plot Profiles
(Johnson & Louis, 1987)

Plot Profiles can help students plot conflict escalation and de-escalation in chapter books, as well as graph the plot development of a story. A Plot Profile is in the form of a graph. On the right side of the graph is a continuum, ranging from low to high. Across the bottom of the graph is the number of each chapter of the book. Students discuss each chapter and together decide the level of

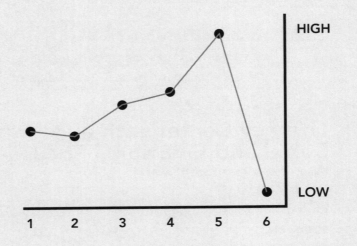

conflict, tension, or excitement in that portion of the text.

STEPS:

1. Select a novel in which there is a great deal of conflict.

2. Devise two Plot Profiles. The first should be large enough for the entire class to see. The second should be a replication of the class plot profile on paper that each student can keep at his desk.

3. Have students read the first chapter. Discuss the level of conflict and/or tension in the plot. As a class, decide how to mark the Plot Profile. Have students mark their own plot profiles.

4. Continue with the same procedure after reading each chapter. Always discuss, as a class, how the Plot Profile should be graphed.

5. At the end of the story, connect the dots to make a line graph. This allows students to see how the plot developed and the impact of the story events on story characters.

Discuss the story as a whole. Focus on how specific events impacted the characters in the story.

"Bookmark"-eting

Students create bookmarks for one another that include a story summary and why they liked the book. Bookmarks should entice other students to read the story.

STEPS:

1. Provide students with a small piece of light-colored tagboard.

2. Ask students to write a few sentences summarizing the book and saying why one of their classmates might want to read the work. Explain that they are trying to "sell" the book, not give away the ending.

Literacy Center with a Social and Emotional Focus
(Morrow & Gambrell, 2004)

Literacy Centers can help children to interact with one another as they read, write, and work creatively to comprehend text.

It is helpful to include numerous books, arranged by genre, with colored tabs on the spine to indicate the category. For example, use red tabs for fairy tales, blue for poetry. Be sure to post a legend on the wall or someplace visible. Some teachers create categories within the fiction genre as well.

Include books that foster social and emotional learning and focus on SEL themes such as problem solving, conflict and conflict escalation, friendship, and bullying. The books listed in this curriculum are good places to start.

Choose books that focus on a theme the class is discussing and display them on open-faced bookshelves so their front covers are visible. Rotate social and emotional learning themes like friendship, feelings, or conflict. Be selective about which books are chosen for display and change them regularly.

After reading a story to the class, put it in the Literacy Center so children can reread or take a "picture walk" through the text. This type of repetition can increase reading fluency.

Include audio versions of selected titles for students who are unable to read the books on their own.

Decorate the area with relevant posters. For example, posters of famous people reading books, strategy overviews like ABCD problem solving, and a chart with ideas for de-escalating conflicts. When setting up the literacy center try to include:

- furniture, such as soft pillows and/or an old couch, that is conducive to reading and working in comfortable surroundings;

- an area for independent reading. Painted refrigerator boxes work well;

- manipulatives such as cutouts of shoe shapes for students to put on when they listen to each other's points of view;

- felt and/or magic magnetic boards with accompanying pieces so that students can reenact and create their own stories;

- open-ended cards. Teachers can write a brief beginning to a story or conflict and laminate it on tagboard. Students can act out the stories/conflict by adding their own ending; and

- puppets.

STRATEGY #15 Thematic Lesson Planning

Teachers can devise their own lessons, discussions, and reflections that focus on character and conflict through literature and the language arts by using the following procedures:

1. Identify themes related to social and emotional learning (SEL), conflict resolution (CR), or character development. Some examples of themes are teasing, friendship, courage, identifying emotion, and managing emotions. Select the theme based on the needs in your classroom, issues in school, or events in the world. Or be proactive and select a theme that you want to teach your students.

2. Identify the purpose of the lesson. Consider what understandings or behaviors you'd like your students to acquire related to this theme. Some examples are: Students will be able to identify...; Students will understand that ...; Students will have more ideas about dealing with..., etc.

3. Identify a few books related to your theme that would help your students explore various aspects of the theme over time. Select one book to start. Ask yourself what SEL/CR/Character messages this book offers.

4. Identify teachings and activities to achieve learning outcomes. Ask yourself:

- What direct SEL skill instruction might students need so you as a teacher can scaffold learning experiences?

- What classroom practices would reinforce the concepts? (For example, using cooperative groups if the theme relates to cooperation, or involving students in problem solving if the theme relates to conflict, and so on.)

- What activities will reinforce the content?

- How might you sequence the lesson? What is your implementation plan for the book and the theme?

Sample Thematic Lesson Planning Sheet

Theme related to conflict, character, social and emotional learning, diversity, etc.:

_____

Title of the book: _____

Specific learning outcomes identified: _____

_____

_____

_____

Skills/ Standards: _____

_____

_____

_____

LESSON OUTLINE:

- Include skill instruction activities or classroom practices to be done before or after a book experience that help achieve outcomes.
- Include questions that are for the whole class, small discussion groups, and/or journal reflections.

Describe the longer implementation plan for your theme and where this story and its accompanying lesson may fall. (Use extra paper if necessary.)

_____

_____

_____

_____

_____

_____

_____

Bibliography

Aldo, A. *Morning Glory Monday.* Toronto: Tundra Books, 2003

Appelt, K. *The Best Kind of Gift.* New York: HarperCollins, 2003

Bang, M. *When Sophie Gets Angry...Really, Really Angry.* New York: Scholastic Paperbacks, 2004

Blume, J. *The Pain and the Great One.* New York: Dragonfly Books, 1985

Bregoli, J. *The Goat Lady.* Gardiner, ME: Tilbury House, 2005

Brisson, P. *The Summer My Father was Ten.* Honesdale, PA: Boyds Mills Press, 1999

Carle, E. *The Grouchy Ladybug.* New York: HarperCollins, 1999

Carlson, N. *How to Lose All Your Friends.* New York: Puffin Books, 1997

Cleary, B. *Dear Mr. Henshaw.* New York: HarperTrophy, 2000

Cosby, B. *Meanest Thing to Say.* New York: Scholastic, 1997

Cosby, B. *The Day I Saw My Father Cry.* New York: Scholastic, 2000

Creech, S. *Love That Dog.* New York: HarperTrophy, 2003

de Paola, T. *Oliver Button is a Sissy.* Orlando, FL: Voyager Books, 1990

Dragonwagon, C. *Bat in the Dining Room.* New York: Marshall Cavendish, 1997

English, K. *Speak to Me (And I Will Listen between the Lines).* New York: Farrar Straus Giroux, 2004

Freymann, S. & Elffers, J. *How Are You Peeling? Foods with Moods.* New York: Scholastic Paperbacks, 2004

Gantos, J. *Joey Pigza Swallowed the Key.* New York: HarperTrophy, 2000

Golenbock, P. *Teammates.* Orlando, FL: Voyager Books, 1992

Grimes, N. *Danitra Brown, Class Clown.* New York: HarperCollins, 2005

Harper, J. *Lizzy's Ups and Downs: Not an Ordinary School Day.* New York: HarperCollins, 2004

Hausman, B. *A to Z: Do You Ever Feel Like Me?: A Guessing Alphabet of Feelings, Words, and Other Cool Stuff.* New York: Dutton, 1999

Henkes, K. *Chester's Way.* New York: HarperTrophy, 1997

Henkes, K. *Chrysanthemum.* New York: HarperTrophy, 1996

Henkes, K. *Owen.* New York: Greenwillow Books, 1993

Henkes, K. *Words of Stone.* New York: HarperTrophy, 2005

Hesse, K. *The Cats in Krasinski Square.* New York: Scholastic, 2004

Hooks, B. *Skin Again.* New York: Hyperion, 2005

Hubbel, P. *Black All Around!* New York: Lee & Low, 2004

Irbinskas, H. *How Jackrabbit Got His Very Long Ears.* Flagstaff, AZ: Northland, 2004

Jones, R.C. *Matthew and Tilly.* New York: Puffin Books, 1995

Johnston, T. *The Harmonica.* Watertown, MA: Charlesbridge, 2004

Joseph, L. *The Color of My Words.* New York: HarperTrophy, 2002

Kellogg, S. *Best Friends.* New York: Puffin Books, 1992

Kellogg, S. *Island of the Skog.* New York: Penguin Young Readers Group, 1993

Kinsey-Warnock, N. *Nora's Ark.* New York: HarperCollins, 2005

Kline, R. *Watch Out for These Weirdos!* New York: Puffin, 1992

Krishnaswami, E. *Chachaji's Cup.* San Francisco, CA: Children's Book Press, 2003

Krull, K. *Harvesting Hope: The Story of Cesar Chavez.* San Diego, CA: Harcourt Children's Books, 2003

Lester, H. *Hooway for Wodney Wat.* New York: Scholastic, 2006, 1999

Lester, J. *From Slave Ship to Freedom Road.* New York: Puffin Books, 1999

Levine, K. *Hana's Suitcase.* Morton Grove, IL: Albert Whitman & Company, 2003

Lionni, L. *It's Mine!* New York: Dragonfly Books, 1996

Lionni, L. *Swimmy.* New York: Dragonfly Books, 1973

Lowry, L. *Taking Care of Terrific.* New York: Yearling, 1984

MacLean, K.L. *Peaceful Piggy Meditation.* Morton Grove, IL: Whitman, 2004

MacLachlan, P. *Through Grandpa's Eyes.* New York: HarperTrophy, 1983

Mobin-Uddin, A. *My Name Is Bilal.* Honesdale, PA: Boyds Mills Press, 2005

Mochizuki, K. *Baseball Saved Us.* New York: Lee & Low Books, 1995

Moss, P. *Say Something.* Gardiner, ME: Tilbury House, 2004

Naylor, P.R. *King of the Playground.* New York: Aladdin Paperbacks, 1994

O'Neill, A. *The Recess Queen.* New York: Scholastic Press, 2002

Perez, A.I. *My Diary from Here to There.* San Francisco: Children's Book Press, 2002

Priest, P. *Pirate's Eye.* Boston: Houghton Mifflin, 2005

Rathmann, P. *Ruby the Copycat.* New York: Scholastic Paperbacks, 1993

Robberecht, T. *Angry Dragon.* New York: Clarion, 2004

Rumford, J. *Nine Animals and the Well.* Boston: Houghton Mifflin, 2003

Scieszka, P. *The True Story of the Three Little Pigs.* New York: Puffin Books, 1996

Shannon, D. *A Bad Case of Stripes.* New York: Scholastic Paperbacks, 2004

Smith, L. *Mrs. Biddlebox.* New York: HarperCollins, 2002

Spinelli, E. *Somebody Loves You, Mr. Hatch.* New York: Aladdin Paperbacks, 1996

Surat, M.M. *Angel Child, Dragon Child.* New York: Scholastic Paperbacks, 1989

Taylor, M.D. *The Well: David's Story.* New York: Dial Books for Young Readers, 1995

Trivizas, E. *The Three Little Wolves and the Big, Bad Pig.* New York: Scholastic, 1994

Turner, P. *The War between the Vowels and the Consonants.* New York: Farrar Straus Giroux, 1999

Tyler, M. *The Skin You Live In.* Chicago, IL: Chicago Children's Museum, 2005

Vail, R. *Sometimes I'm Bombalo.* New York: Scholastic, 2005

Wood, D. *A Quiet Place.* New York: Aladdin, 2005

Woodson, J. *The Other Side of the Fence.* New York: Putnam Juvenile, 2001

Weigelt, U. Translated by James, J. A. *What Lies on the Other Side?* New York: North-South, 2002

Williams, B. *Albert's Impossible Toothache.* Cambridge, MA: Candlewick Press, 2003, 1974

Williams, V.B. *A Chair for My Mother.* New York: HarperTrophy, 1984

References

Cunningham, P.M. (2000). *Phonics they use: Words for reading and writing* (3rd ed.). New York: HarperCollins.

Durlak, J. A., & Weissberg, R. P. (2007). *The impact of after-school programs that seek to promote personal and social skills.* *Retrieved August 2007. CASEL, University of Illinois at Chicago. http://www.casel.org/downloads/ASP-Full.pdf.

Gambrell, L.B. & Bales, R.J. (1986). Mental imagery and the comprehension-monitoring of fourth- and fifth grade poor readers. *Reading Research Quarterly*, 21, 454-464.

Goleman, D. (1997). *Emotional intelligence: Why it can matter more than IQ.* New York, Bantam.

Greenberg, M. T., Weissberg, R. P., O'Brien, M. U., Zins, J. E., Fredericks, L., Resnik, H., & Elias, M. J. (2003). Enhancing school-based prevention and youth development through coordinated social, emotional, and academic learning. *American Psychologist, 58*, 466-474.

Harste, J.C., Short, K.G., & Burke, C. (1988). *Creating Classrooms for Authors.* Portsmouth: Heinemann.

Head, M.H. & Readence J.E. (1986). Anticipation reaction guides: Meaning through prediction. In J.E. Readence & D.W. Moore (Eds.), *Reading in the content areas* (2nd) Ed., (pp 229-234). Dubuque, IA: Kendall/Hunt.

Heimlich J.E., & Pitman, S.D, (1986). *Semantic mapping: Classroom applications.* Newark, DE: International Reading Association.

Johnson T.D. & Louis, D.R. (1987) *Literacy through literature.* Portsmouth, NH: Heinemann.

Macon, J.M., Bewell. D., & Vogt, M.E. (1991). *Responses to literature*, grades K-8. Newark, DE: International Reading Association.

Maslow, A.H. (1943). A theory of human motivation. *Psychological Review*, 50, 370-396.

Morrow, L. M. and Gambrell, L.G. (2004). *Using Children's Literature in Preschool: Comprehending and Enjoying Books in Using Children's Literature Throughout the Preschool Curriculum.* Newark: Delaware: International Reading Association.

Pressley, M., El-Dinary, P.B., Gaskins, I., Schuder, T., Bergman, J., Almasi, J., et al. (1992). Beyond direct explanation: Transactional instruction of reading comprehension strategies. *The Elementary School Journal, 92*, 511–555.

Pressley, M., Johnson, C.J., Symons, S., McGoldrick, J.A., & Kurita, J.A. (1989). Strategies that improve children's memory and comprehension of text. *The Elementary School Journal, 90*, 3–32.

Roser, N. & Martinez, N. (eds.) (1995). Language charts: A record of storytime talk. In Roser N., & Hoffman. *Book Talk and Beyond.* Newark: Delaware.

Tompkins, G.E. (2003). *Literacy in the twenty-first century: Teaching reading and writing in pre-kindergarten through grade 4.* Upper Saddle River: New Jersey: Pearson Education, Inc.

Stauffer, R.G. (1975). *Directing the reading-thinking process.* New York: Harper & Row.

Zins, J. E., Weissberg, R. P., Wang, M. C., & Walberg. H. J. (Eds.). (2004). *Building academic success on social and emotional learning: What does the research say?* New York: Teachers College Press.

Notes

Notes